Mahsa Jenabi

PrIME

Mahsa Jenabi

PrIME

Primitive Interaction Tasks for Multi-Display Environments

Südwestdeutscher Verlag für Hochschulschriften

Impressum/Imprint (nur für Deutschland/only for Germany)
Bibliografische Information der Deutschen Nationalbibliothek: Die Deutsche Nationalbibliothek verzeichnet diese Publikation in der Deutschen Nationalbibliografie; detaillierte bibliografische Daten sind im Internet über http://dnb.d-nb.de abrufbar.

Alle in diesem Buch genannten Marken und Produktnamen unterliegen warenzeichen-, marken- oder patentrechtlichem Schutz bzw. sind Warenzeichen oder eingetragene Warenzeichen der jeweiligen Inhaber. Die Wiedergabe von Marken, Produktnamen, Gebrauchsnamen, Handelsnamen, Warenbezeichnungen u.s.w. in diesem Werk berechtigt auch ohne besondere Kennzeichnung nicht zu der Annahme, dass solche Namen im Sinne der Warenzeichen- und Markenschutzgesetzgebung als frei zu betrachten wären und daher von jedermann benutzt werden dürften.

Coverbild: www.ingimage.com

Verlag: Südwestdeutscher Verlag für Hochschulschriften GmbH & Co. KG
Heinrich-Böcking-Str. 6-8, 66121 Saarbrücken, Deutschland
Telefon +49 681 37 20 271-1, Telefax +49 681 37 20 271-0
Email: info@svh-verlag.de

Approved by: Konstanz, Uni,Diss.,2011

Herstellung in Deutschland:
Schaltungsdienst Lange o.H.G., Berlin
Books on Demand GmbH, Norderstedt
Reha GmbH, Saarbrücken
Amazon Distribution GmbH, Leipzig
ISBN: 978-3-8381-3079-8

Imprint (only for USA, GB)
Bibliographic information published by the Deutsche Nationalbibliothek: The Deutsche Nationalbibliothek lists this publication in the Deutsche Nationalbibliografie; detailed bibliographic data are available in the Internet at http://dnb.d-nb.de.

Any brand names and product names mentioned in this book are subject to trademark, brand or patent protection and are trademarks or registered trademarks of their respective holders. The use of brand names, product names, common names, trade names, product descriptions etc. even without a particular marking in this works is in no way to be construed to mean that such names may be regarded as unrestricted in respect of trademark and brand protection legislation and could thus be used by anyone.

Cover image: www.ingimage.com

Publisher: Südwestdeutscher Verlag für Hochschulschriften GmbH & Co. KG
Heinrich-Böcking-Str. 6-8, 66121 Saarbrücken, Germany
Phone +49 681 37 20 271-1, Fax +49 681 37 20 271-0
Email: info@svh-verlag.de

Printed in the U.S.A.
Printed in the U.K. by (see last page)
ISBN: 978-3-8381-3079-8

Copyright © 2012 by the author and Südwestdeutscher Verlag für Hochschulschriften GmbH & Co. KG and licensors
All rights reserved. Saarbrücken 2012

Contents

Acknowledgements   xxi

Abstract   xxiii

Zusammenfassung   xxvii

Publications   xxxi

1 Introduction   1
    1.1 Motivation 1
    1.2 Research Assumptions 2
    1.3 Contributions of the Thesis 4
       1.3.1 Theoretical Part 4
       1.3.2 Practical Part 5
    1.4 Thesis Outline 6

2 Related work   9
    2.1 Mobile Device Interaction 9
    2.2 Multi-Display Environments 14

2.3 MDE Requirements 22

2.4 Object Selection and Movement Methods in MDEs . 24

    2.4.1 Slingshot 26

    2.4.2 Pick and Drop 26

    2.4.3 Hyperdragging 26

    2.4.4 Lift and Drop 27

    2.4.5 Drag and Pop 29

    2.4.6 Drag and Pick 29

2.5 Summary of the Chapter 31

3 Theory 33

3.1 Displays 33

3.2 Single-Display Interaction 34

    3.2.1 Primitive Interaction Tasks for Single-Display Environments 34

    3.2.2 ISO 9241-400 List of Primitive Tasks 37

3.3 Multi-Display Interaction 38

    3.3.1 Object Selection 40

    3.3.2 Object Transfer 42

    3.3.3 Focusing-Brushing-Linking in Collaborative MDEs 42

    3.3.4 Visualization Gallery 46

3.4 PrIME Diagrammatic Notations 47

    3.4.1 State Transition Networks 47

	3.4.2	PrIME Diagrams	49
3.5	Summary of the Chapter		53

4 Single-Display Interaction: CloudBrowsing Project   55

4.1	Introduction		55
4.2	Requirement Engineering		57
4.3	Technical Set-up		57
	4.3.1	Media Room	58
	4.3.2	PanoramaLab at the ZKM	58
4.4	Design Process		60
	4.4.1	Prototype 1	61
		Design	61
		Implementation	66
		Evaluation	67
	4.4.2	Prototype 2	69
		Design	69
		Evaluation	70
		Result	70
	4.4.3	Prototype 3	73
		Design	73
		Preliminary Evaluation in the Museum . . .	74
		Interdisciplinary User study in the Museum	75
4.5	Lessons Learned		78

	4.6	Summary of the Chapter	80
5	**Methodology**	**81**
	5.1	Media Room Setting	82
	5.2	Input Devices for MDEs	83
	5.3	Display Recognition	85
	5.4	Technical Infrastructure	85
	5.5	System Architecture	86
	5.6	Experimental Approach	89
	5.7	Summary of the Chapter	91
6	**Multi-Display Interaction: PrIME Project**	**93**
	6.1	Introduction	93
	6.2	iPhone Interaction Design	94
		6.2.1 CoverFlow Visualization	95
		6.2.2 DisplayMap Visualization	95
		6.2.3 ZoomGrid Visualization	96
		6.2.4 Comparison between the GUIs	97
		6.2.5 Object Ordering Algorithms	97
		CoverFlow Ordering Approaches	99
		ZoomGrid Visualization	100
	6.3	Experiment 1: GUI Battle	102
		6.3.1 Experiment Design	103

		6.3.2	Results 104

- 6.3.2 Results 104
- 6.3.3 Discussion 109
- 6.4 Bridging the Gap between Displays 111
- 6.5 Laser-pointing Device Interaction Design 113
- 6.6 The iPhone vs. the Laser-Pointing Device 115
- 6.7 Experiment 2: Input Devices Battle 116
  - 6.7.1 Experiment Design 116
  - 6.7.2 Results 121
  - 6.7.3 Subjective Feedback 122
  - 6.7.4 Discussion 125
  - 6.7.5 Limitations of the Interaction Technique . . . 126
    - Scalability 126
    - Multi-User Control 127
    - Objects on the Display 127
    - Visual Discriminability 127
- 6.8 Summary of the Chapter 128

7 MDE's Application Domain   129

- 7.1 Application Scenarios 129
- 7.2 Brainstorming 130
- 7.3 CrossStorm Prototype 131
  - 7.3.1 Interaction Scenario 132
  - 7.3.2 Design Decisions 135

		7.3.3	Advantages of the System 137

       7.3.4   Future Work 138

  7.4   Summary of the Chapter 142

8 Thesis Conclusions and Future Work   **143**

  8.1   Conclusion 143

       8.1.1   Practical Contribution 143

       8.1.2   Theoretical Contribution 146

  8.2   Future Work 148

               Extending the List of Primitive Interaction Tasks 148

               Extending to Further Interaction Primitives . 148

               Mixed Multiple Display and Non-Display Devices 149

               Semantic Relationships 149

               Universal Remote Controller vs. Integrated Member of MDE 149

               Attention Management 149

A CloudBrowsing Credits   **151**

  A.1   Credits 153

  A.2   Reference 154

B CloudBrowsing Help Instruction   **155**

C PrIME Experiment 2 Tasks   **157**

Bibliography 161

List of Figures

1.1 Evolution of spatially continuous workspaces 3

2.1 The sweep technique can be used to control a cursor 11

2.2 Interaction with the SnapAndGrab display 12

2.3 An orientation-aware handheld 12

2.4 The user holds up a tablet PC in front of a projected image 13

2.5 A handheld device as a chameleon 13

2.6 LensMouse 14

2.7 i-Land project 15

2.8 Cristal project 16

2.9 WeSpace project 16

2.10 A screenshot of the IMPROMPTU user interface . . 17

2.11 The privacy menu in IMPROMPTU 17

2.12 A screen shot of the Dynamo setting 18

2.13 Stitching technique 18

2.14 Multi-device, multi-user adaptation of Google Earth 19

2.15 Deskotheque setup with multiple projections 20

2.16 Deskotheque using Caleydo application [Streit et al., 2009]. 20

2.17 TouchProjector project 21

2.18 The user is interacting across displays with UIC . . 21

2.19 A screen shot of the G-stalt project [Zigelbaum et al., 2010]. 22

2.20 Slingshot and Pantograph 26

2.21 Pick and Drop method 27

2.22 Hyperdragging method 28

2.23 Hyperdragging scenario 28

2.24 Lift and Drop technique 29

2.25 Drag and Pop technique 30

2.26 Drag and pick technique 31

3.1 Task hierarchies for 1D, 2D, and 3D position tasks . 37

3.2 The boundaries of the PrIME set 38

3.3 Object selection with abstract objects 40

3.4 Object selection using an iPhone 41

3.5 Object selection using a laser-pointing device 41

3.6 Object transfer using an iPhone 43

3.7 Objects transfer from one display to another by keeping a link to the original display 45

3.8 Visualization gallery using an iPhone 46

List of Figures

3.9   A state transition diagram for a drawing tool 47

3.10 A hierarchical state transition diagram for a drawing tool 48

3.11 Interaction dialogue with multiple displays to perform primitive tasks 49

3.12 state transition network for performing object-selection tasks 50

3.13 state transition network for performing object-transfer tasks 51

3.14 state transition network for performing focus-brush-link task tasks 52

3.15 state transition network for performing visualization gallery tasks 53

4.1   The PanoramaScreen at the ZKM 56

4.2   The input device is a black case that includes an iPod Touch or iPhone and an orientation sensor called inertia cube sensor. 58

4.3   The Media Room at the University of Konstanz ... 59

4.4   Eyevis Cube displays 59

4.5   Primary evaluation of the CloudBrowsing prototype 59

4.6   Input device in the ZKM Museum 60

4.7   CloudBrowsing installation in ZKM museum 61

4.8   Pointing to an image of interest 62

4.9   User Interface (UI) of the iPhone in the pointing mode 63

4.10 GUI for searching keywords 63

4.11	Search results	63
4.12	Related images on the iPhone	64
4.13	GUI for the Wikipedia page	65
4.14	Two design prototypes for presenting the hyperlinks	66
4.15	The final version of how to show the hyperlinks on the iPhone.	66
4.16	This figure show the area outside the installation room	67
4.17	This figure illustrates the architecture of the CloudBrowsing.	67
4.18	CoverFlow visualization of the related images	68
4.19	Diagram: Awareness of the functionalities	71
4.20	Diagram: tiredness of the device	72
4.21	Visible controls were added to the GUI	73
4.22	A dummy screenshot of the iPhone	74
4.23	Result of the questionnaire data: positive factors	77
4.24	Result of the questionnaire data: negative factors	77
5.1	The iPhone and the laser-pointing device with markers.	82
5.2	The Optitrack cameras in the Media Room	83
5.3	Squidy library	86
5.4	Tracking data from the Optitrack system	87
5.5	The pipeline runs on the Microsoft Surface display	88
5.6	System architecture	90

List of Figures   xiii

5.7 Space distribution of the landscape between the three displays 90

6.1 CoverFlow GUI for selecting objects 94

6.2 Window selection for iPhone 95

6.3 DisplayMap GUI for selecting objects 96

6.4 ZoomGrid GUI for selecting objects 96

6.5 Z-Order Curve illustrated for four iterations. 99

6.6 Hilbert Curve first order. 100

6.7 Hilbert Curve's second order 100

6.8 This figure shows the result of applying the PixelMap Density approach on the objects inside the display. 102

6.9 This figure shows the result of applying the PixelMap Left To Right approach on the objects inside the display. On the iPhone the objects with ordering from 8 to 39 are shown. 103

6.10 The user is selecting objects from the Eyevis Cube display 105

6.11 Mean task completion time for all the 7 GUIs 106

6.12 Mean error rate for all the 7 GUIs 108

6.13 This diagram shows the mean coverage rate for all the 7 GUIs 108

6.14 iPhone clipboard view 112

6.15 display filtering functionality for iPhone 112

6.16 Tasks menu for iPhone 113

6.17 laser-pointing device 113

6.18	Right-click menu for the laser-pointing device	114
6.19	Experiment 2: Object transfer using an iPhone	118
6.20	Experiment 2: Object selection using an iPhone	119
6.21	Experiment 2: Object transfer using a laser-pointing device	119
6.22	Experiment 2: Object selection using a laser-pointing device	120
6.23	Diagram: iPhone and laser-pointing device	123
7.1	Team Storm tool	131
7.2	Electronic brainstorming system	132
7.3	CrossStorm: The moderator is explaining the problem.	133
7.4	CrossStrom: moderator has created post-its on the display	133
7.5	CrossStrom:user creates post-its on the display	134
7.6	CrossStorm prototype: a screenshot of the iPhone GUI for writing post-its.	135
7.7	CrossStorm prototype: a screenshot of the editor	135
7.8	CrossStorm: makers attached to the iPhone	135
7.9	CrossStorm scenario	136
7.10	This is a screenshot of the Menu items	136
7.11	Display icon showed on the iPhone GUI	136
7.12	Microsoft Surface icon is shown as a display on focus	136
7.13	Feedback for object selection	137

List of Figures

7.14 CrossStorm scenario in the Media Room 138

7.15 CrossStorm scenario with the moderator and two users 139

7.16 Object positioning mode 139

7.17 Interaction with the Cube display 140

7.18 Brainstorming diagram 141

7.19 Maximum number of post-its, that are readable . . . 141

8.1 Contribution of the thesis 147

B.1 CloudBrowsing Guidance 156

List of Tables

2.1 This table compares the related works according to the MDE requirements criteria 25

3.1 This table lists the task primitives for single displays according to the ISO 9241-400 in the first column. The second column presents the similar task according to the Foley's list. The third column provides some comments about this comparison. . . 37

4.1 The table lists the means and standard deviations of navigation possibilities. 76

5.1 The above table compares potential input devices for multi-display environments. 92

6.1 This table lists the advantages and disadvantages of CoverFlow, ZoomGrid, and DisplayMap GUIs. . 98

6.2 Standard deviations of the task completion time for three different ordering algorithms 105

6.3 Standard deviations of the task completion time for ZoomGrid visualization 105

List of Tables

6.4 This table lists the mean and standard deviations of the task completion time for the DisplayMap, CoverFlow and ZoomGrid GUI. The type of ordering algorithm is ignored here, therefore, the average of the values for different algorithms are considered for each type of GUI. 106

6.5 This table lists the mean and standard deviations of the error rate in the DisplayMap, CoverFlow and ZoomGrid GUI as the number of errors. The type of ordering algorithm was ignored here, therefore, the average of the values for different algorithms were considered for each GUI type. . . 107

6.6 This table lists the means and standard deviations of the error rate for three different ordering algorithms with the CoverFlow visualization as the number of errors. 107

6.7 This table lists the means and standard deviations of the error rate for three different ordering algorithms with the ZoomGrid visualization as the number of errors. 109

6.8 This table lists the mean and standard deviations of the coverage rate in the DisplayMap, CoverFlow and ZoomGrid GUI (the range is from 0 to 1, where 1 means 100% of the task was completed). The type of ordering algorithm is ignored here, therefore, the average of the values for different algorithms are considered for each GUI type. 109

6.9 This table lists the means and standard deviations of the coverage rate for three different ordering algorithms with the CoverFlow visualization (the range is from 0 to 1, where 1 means 100% of the task was completed). 109

6.10 This table lists the means and standard deviations of the coverage rate for three different ordering algorithms with the ZoomGrid visualization (the range is from 0 to 1, where 1 means 100% of the task was completed). 110

List of Tables

6.11 This table lists the mean and standard deviations of the task completion time for the two tasks of the first hypothesis. 122

6.12 This table lists the mean and standard deviations of the task completion time for the two tasks of hypothesis two. 122

6.13 This table lists the mean and standard deviations of the task completion time for the task of overlapping object, hypothesis three. The standard deviation for iPhone is relatively high. The reason is that one user took much longer to accomplish the task than others. Other users finished the task in less than 29 seconds, but this user took 129 seconds. The backup video shows that the user was confused in the beginning and therefore played around with the device for a while before starting the task. 123

Acknowledgements

I would like to thank all those who kindly offered me their professional and emotional support through out this research.

First, many thanks to my advisor, Prof. Harald Reiterer for giving me the opportunity to do my PhD at the HCI group of the University of Konstanz. His valuable comments and suggestions helped me to successfully finish my PhD in three years.

I would like to thank my second advisor, Prof. Oliver Deussen, for his interest in my thesis and also for his feedback. Furthermore, many thanks to Prof. Daniel Keim for his suggestions on the algorithms used in this research. I also thank him for accepting the role of committee chair at my PhD defense.

This PhD work would not have been possible without the financial support by the German Research Society (DFG) under the grant GK-1042, *Explorative Analysis and Visualization of Large Information Spaces*, University of Konstanz.

My colleagues at the HCI group have also played an important role in this research through their comments and suggestions. I would like to thank all the professors of the Informatics and Information Technology department at the University of Konstanz, as well as the GK advisors, especially Prof. Dietmar Saupe for his guidance, feedback and support. Many thanks also to the GK PhD students, the GK secretary and administrator, Philipp Ziemer, Florian Junghanns, as well as Prof. Alan Dix, Prof. Ulrik Brandes, Dr. Katrin Allmendinger, Jens Gerken, Hans-Christian Jetter, Ulrike Pfeil, Johannes Schult and Dr. Florin Mansmann for reviewing my work. Special thanks to my students who accompanied me during my PhD and contributed to the success of the projects: Marcio Alves de Castro, Stephanie

Höhn, Simon Fäh in PriME project, and Markus Nitsche in CloudBrowsing project.

I would also like to acknowledge all the contributors to the CloudBrowsing project, which was a cooperation project between the HCI group of the University of Konstanz and ZKM museum of art and media. Special thanks to Bernd Lintermann, the Head of the Institute for Visual Media at ZKM and to Katrin Allmendinger for the excellent team work in designing and conducting user studies, and to our project team at the University of Konstanz, Werner König and Markus Nitsche.

My sincere gratitude also goes to Prof. Jan Borchers for introducing me to the field of HCI and also to Tico Ballagas for inspiring me to the world of Mobile Interaction. Thank you also to Prof. Faramarz Samavati, my first professor in Computer Science, who encouraged me to continue in this branch of science.

Many thanks to Laura Sghendo, Michael Spagnol, Dominika Metelski and Dr. Tim Fischer for proof-reading the thesis and to Thorsten Karrer for the nice LATEXtemplate.

I would not have gotten so far without the love and support of my parents, Minoo Imanian and Ali Jenabi and my lovely brothers, Aria and Pooya Jenabi. They encouraged me during my whole life and I am proud of having them always by my side. Finally, I wish to express my gratitude to Tim Fischer for his love and support and for always being there for me. He helped me remember my aims and encouraged me to work hard in order to achieve them.

God! Thank you for everything!

Abstract

Multiple displays are commonly used in meetings and discussion rooms. These settings provide new challenges for designing fluid interaction across displays. For instance, a list of primitive interaction tasks in such environments has not been investigated in literature. In addition, past researchers have carried out their research using mobile phones as input devices to control displays. However, it is still unclear whether an input device with an integrated display can improve the performance of multi-display interaction tasks.

This research contributes to the design space of the multi-display environments (MDE) in two aspects. Its first contribution is theoretical, as it lists the primitive interaction tasks for MDEs. The indicated primitive tasks are: object selection, object transfer and focusing-brushing-linking in collaborative MDE, as well as visualization gallery as an extension to the list of primitive tasks for single-display interaction. This list helps interaction designers, who design new input devices, to be aware of the tasks that the device should support. Furthermore, it can be used as criteria to evaluate novel input devices.

The second contribution of this research is practical and it is aimed at answering the following research questions, which the state-of-the-art techniques have left unanswered.

Does a mobile input device with an integrated display improve performing cross-display interaction tasks?
The idea behind this research was to compare two devices, one of which has an integrated display whereas the other does not.

To answer the research question, a working prototype, called PrIME prototype, was implemented. This was done using a laser-pointing device and an iPhone as two alternative input devices for MDEs.

A user study was conducted to compare these devices according to their performance, as well as for the users' subjective feedback. The outcome of the experiment indicated that the iPhone is better suited at selecting overlapping objects, objects that are small, and objects which are at a distance. Although it was hypothesized that the laser-pointing device might be quicker than the iPhone to select larger objects, the paired sampling t-test did not prove any significant difference between the two.

Transferring one object from one display to another was significantly quicker using the iPhone. Surprisingly, the iPhone was not quicker at transferring more objects from one display to two other displays. In fact, the result of the t-test showed no significant difference. It was expected that the iPhone would be quicker in performing more complex tasks, namely where several tasks are done one after another. This was assumed given that the iPhone has a clipboard which can save the selected objects and which the user can carry around.

The users' subjective feedback showed that the iPhone was considered significantly better than the laser-pointing device. This is because it was regarded as easier to use, more accurate for object selection, less tiring to carry and it also responded quicker to the users' input.

Using an iPhone as an input device to control a large display, which GUI and which ordering algorithm would be the most preferable according to the users' performance and subjective feedback?
Three different visualizations were implemented, namely CoverFlow, ZoomGrid and DisplayMap. For the last two visualizations, three different algorithms were used to put objects in order. Therefore, each user tested seven different conditions. A user study was conducted to compare these seven conditions. As the result of the experiment indicated, CoverFlow visualization is significantly slower than the other two GUIs,

therefore, it is not appropriate for these sort of tasks.

DisplayMap and ZoomGrid were both similarly fast. In fact, no significant difference was indicated. According to the subjective feedback by the users, the ZoomGrid GUI was preferable, because it showed a good overview of the existing objects.

What application domain can benefit from the PrIME prototype?
To show the application of the PrIME prototype concept in a real life scenario, CrossStorm prototype was implemented. CrossStorm supports users in brainstorming sessions. Users can make, delete, and move the post-its across displays using an iPhone as an input device. This prototype allowed two users to use two iPhones simultaneously, which gave users the possibility of using more iPhones to share their ideas with other members of their group.

Lessons learned from the design and implementation of these prototypes showed the impacts of using a mobile input device with an integrated display for cross-display interaction.

Zusammenfassung

Sowohl im unternehmerischen als auch im universitären Bereich kommen zur Unterstützung interaktiver Arbeitssituationen sogenannte Multi-Display-Umgebungen immer häufiger zum Einsatz. Dabei werden mehrere Bildschirmgeräte meist ganz unterschiedlicher Art und Größe verwendet, die so vernetzt sind, dass sie miteinander interagieren können. So können z.B. Objekte von einem Bildschirm auf einen anderen bewegt werden. Daher eignet sich eine Multi-Display-Umgebung u.a. insbesondere für interaktive Gruppenarbeit.

Solche interaktiven Umgebungen stellen den Interaktionsdesigner vor einige Herausforderungen, insbesondere in Hinblick auf die reibungslose Zusammenarbeit der verschiedenen Bildschirmgeräte untereinander. Bis heute ist jedoch noch nicht untersucht worden, welche Interaktionsaufgaben dabei überhaupt eine wichtige Rolle spielen.

Darüber hinaus ist die Verwendung von Mobiltelefonen als Eingabegeräte für größere Bildschirme zwar gegenwärtig Thema vieler Veröffentlichungen, jedoch wurde bisher noch nicht untersucht, ob ein Eingabegerät mit integriertem Bildschirm die Ausführung von Interaktionsaufgaben zwischen verschiedenen Displays verbessern kann.

Die vorliegende Arbeit deckt zwei Bereiche des Interaktionsdesigns für Multi-Display-Umgebungen ab. Als erstes wird im theoretischen Teil ein Satz primitiver Interaktionsaufgaben vorgestellt. Dieser beinhaltet folgende Aufgaben: Objektauswahl, Objektverschiebung sowie Fokus, Brushing und Linking in kollaborativen Multi-Display-Umgebungen.

Durch den vorgestellten Aufgabensatz erhält der Interaktionsdesigner eine Vorgabe, welche Interaktionsaufgaben beim Entwurf neuer Eingabegeräte für Multi-Display-Umgebungen am wichtigsten sind. Weiterhin kann diese Liste auch als Kriterium für die Evaluation von Eingabegeräten hilfreich sein.

Im zweiten, experimentellen Teil wird der vorher definierte Aufgabensatz genutzt, um folgende Forschungsfragen zu adressieren, die durch die aktuelle Forschung bisher nicht bearbeitet worden sind:

Kann ein mobiles Eingabegerät mit integriertem Bildschirm die Ausführung von primitiven Interaktionsaufgaben in einer Multi-Display-Umgebung verbessern?

Um diese Fragestellung zu beantworten, wurden zwei Eingabegeräte, je eines mit und eines ohne Bildschirm, prototypisch implementiert und gegenüber gestellt. Dazu wurden im Prototyp PrIME ein iPhone und ein spezieller Laserpointer als potenzielle Eingabegeräte genutzt. Die Performanz der Geräte wurde verglichen, außerdem wurde in einer Benutzerstudie die Akzeptanz der Benutzer erfragt.

Das Ergebnis dieser Studie hat gezeigt, dass das iPhone besser geeignet ist, um überlappende, kleine oder weit entfernte Objekte auszuwählen. Obwohl in der Hypothese angenommen wurde, dass das iPhone für die Auswahl großer Objekte schneller als der Laserpointer wäre, wurde im Pair Sampling T-Test kein signifikanter Unterschied zwischen den beiden Eingabegeräten gefunden.

Bei der Verschiebung einzelner Objekte von einem Bildschirm zum anderen war die Verwendung des iPhones signifikant schneller. Im Gegensatz dazu wurde für das Verschieben mehrerer Objekte von einem Bildschirm auf zwei weitere kein Geschwindigkeitsvorteil ermittelt. Dies ist insofern überraschend, weil zuvor angenommen wurde, dass komplexe Aufgaben schneller mit dem iPhone auszuführen wären, da alle ausgewählten Objekte im Clipboard zu sehen waren.

Die Benutzerbefragung ergab, dass das iPhone als signifikant besser empfunden wurde. Als Gründe wurden angegeben: einfachere Bedienung, präzisere Objektauswahl, bessere Handlichkeit und schnellere Rückmeldung zu Benutzereingaben.

Welche grafischen Benutzeroberflächen und Anordnungsalgorithmen werden vom Benutzer bevorzugt und sind bezüglich der Performanz geeigneter, um große Bildschirme per iPhone fern zu steuern?

Für diese Forschungsfrage wurden drei verschiedene Visualisierungstypen implementiert: CoverFlow, ZoomGrid und DisplayMap. Für ZoomGrid und CoverFlow sind jeweils drei verschiedene Anordnungsalgorithmen verwendet worden. Im Rahmen einer Benutzerstudie wurden jeweils alle sieben Benutzer-oberflächen getestet. Das Ergebnis zeigt, dass CoverFlow im Vergleich zu den anderen beiden Visualisierungstypen signifikant langsamer und daher für solche Aufgaben nicht geeignet ist.

Zwischen DisplayMap und ZoomGrid ist jedoch kein signifikanter Unterschied bezüglich der Performanz festgestellt worden. Die Benutzerbefragung ergab eine Präferenz für ZoomGrid, was mit der gesteigerten Übersichtlichkeit der Objektanzeige begründet wurde.

Welche Anwendungsbereiche können vom PrIME-Prototyp profitieren?

Die Umsetzung des PrIME-Konzepts in realen Situationen wurde mit der Implementierung des CrossStorm Prototyps geschaffen. CrossStorm hat zur Aufgabe, Benutzer bei Brainstorming-Sitzungen zu unterstützen.

Benutzer können ihr iPhone verwenden, um Post-Its (Notizzettel) zu generieren, zu löschen oder zwischen Bildschirmen zu verschieben. Dieser Prototyp erlaubt die gleichzeitige Interaktion zweier Nutzer mit jeweils einem iPhone. Im Vergleich zu der Manipulation durch ein einzelnes iPhone erleichtert dies den Austausch von Ideen in einer Arbeitsgruppe.

Das vorliegende Ergebnis zeigt, welche Vorteile ein Eingabegerät mit integriertem Bildschirm in Multi-Display-Umgebungen bietet.

Publications

Papers

Jenabi, M., Reiterer, H., *Primitive Interaction Tasks for Multi-Display Environments (PrIME): A hands-on approach*, In Proceedings of the International Conference on Advanced Visual Interfaces (AVI '10), Giuseppe Santucci (Ed.). ACM, New York, NY, USA, 412, 2010

Jenabi, M., *PrIME -Primitive Interaction Tasks for Multi-Display Environments*. In Proceedings of the Joint Workshop of the German Research Training Groups in Computer Science. 2010, Holz, Ribe- Baumann, Bruckner (Ed.). GITO mbH Verlag, pp. 24, 2010.

Jenabi, M., *Multimodal interaction with mobile phones*, Gemeinsamer Workshop der Informatik-Graduiertenkollegs und Forschungskollegs 2009, Avanes, A., Fahland, D., Geibig, J., Haschemi, S., Heglmeier, S., Sadilek, D., Theisselmann, F., Wachsmuth, G., Weissleder, S. (eds.) , pp. 26, 2009.

Museum Installation

CloudBrowsing installation in ZKM museum Karlsruhe, Germany (Bernd Lintermann, Torsten Belschner, Mahsa Jenabi, Werner A. König: CloudBrowsing (2008-09), (c) ZKM — Karlsruhe)

Further Publication

Jenabi, M., Reiterer, H., *Finteraction - Finger interaction with mobile phone*, Workshop on Future Mobile Experiences (NordiCHI), Lund, Sweden, October 2008.

Chapter 1

Introduction

"More time is wasted in front of computers than on highways."

—Ben Shneiderman, From Universal Usability, 2000

1.1 Motivation

Meeting rooms are nowadays increasingly equipped with many displays of different sizes and with a variety of functionalities (such as, touch sensitivity). While large displays are suitable for presentation, horizontal touch tables, such as Microsoft Surface, may enhance collaborative work. In addition, people often bring their own Tablet PCs and/or mobile phones, which also have integrated displays. This results in "coupled displays" [Terrenghi et al., 2009] in the room, introducing new challenges for cross-display interaction.

<small>Coupled displays</small>

Multiple displays are beneficial in collaborative work, or presentation sessions. For example, during a presentation meeting, one might want to show data about accidents in one particular year and also show the geographical locations of these accidents through Google Earth on another display simultaneously. Further displays could show a table of accident costs and impacts. Even though in most cases such a multi visualization option is possible when the displays are all

<small>Advantages of multiple displays</small>

connected to the same computer, the configuration of views is time-consuming. An intuitive interaction method is required in these situations.

<small>large single display vs. multiple displays</small>

One might argue that a single large display can also be used instead of multiple displays to view multiple visualizations by means of multiple windows. But, in collaborative scenarios such as workshops that people have to work simultaneously in subgroups more than one display is necessary (at least one display for each subgroup). In addition, regarding privacy issues using more than one display is inevitable, since each user might have a different role, therefore, different access/view rights to the data. Private displays, such as mobile phones or Tablet PCs are necessary for writing notes for example in meeting sessions.

<small>Within-display interaction vs. between-display interaction</small>

Interaction in MDEs can be divided into two types, namely within-display interaction and between-display interaction. Within-display interaction includes the method of interaction well-known from single-display workspaces. Users should be able to move and manipulate objects inside the display. A set of primitive interaction tasks is mentioned in ISO 9241-400 and [Foley et al., 1984]. Between-display interaction (also known as cross-display interaction) includes a specific set of interaction tasks that can only be performed, when two or more coupled displays are available; such as when transferring an object from one display to another. Between-display interaction is a challenge for HCI researchers and interaction designers. This type of interaction is the focus of this research.

1.2 Research Assumptions

The following are the conditions which were assumed for this research.

Multi-Display
The interactive room includes more than two interactive displays, which can also be located at a distance. These displays can be normal monitors, high-resolution large public displays, or small personal devices such as PDAs or mobile phones (see figure 1.1 below).

1.2 Research Assumptions

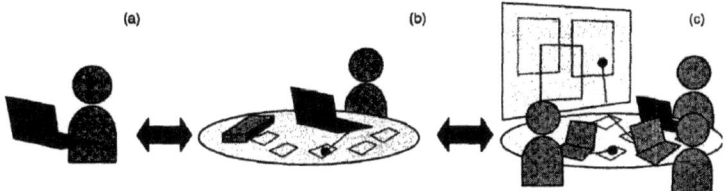

Figure 1.1: Evolution of spatially continuous workspaces: (a) A user can perform individual tasks with a portable computer.(b) The table becomes an extension of the portable computer. (c) Pre-installed computer displays (table and wall) also serve as shared workspaces for collaborative tasks (reference: [Rekimoto and Saitoh, 1999]).

Multi-User
There are many projects investigating multi-display solutions for single users (for example, the multi-monitor system [Forlines et al., 2006]). The focus of this research project is on multi-user multi-display environments that support teamwork. Therefore, the single-user scenarios are not considered.

Co-Located
The cooperation between users is co-located. This means that systems using video conferencing for remote communication, although interesting in their own right, go beyond the scope of this research.

Audience
The audience are over 10 years of age, and do not suffer from special disabilities. The system may still be applicable to many kinds of disabilities, but no special policies are considered for barrier freedom.

Cross-Display Interaction
As mentioned earlier, there are two types of interaction in MDEs: within-display interaction and between-display interaction. The focus of this research is only on between-display interaction.

1.3 Contributions of the Thesis

This thesis contributed to both the theoretical and the practical parts of the HCI.

1.3.1 Theoretical Part

In the first part of this research, a list of primitive kinds of between-display interaction are indicated. These tasks are inspired by example applications mentioned in chapter 2. The primitive tasks are as follows.

Primitive interaction tasks

- Object selection: Selecting one or more objects from one or more displays, for example, for collecting objects of interest from different displays to drop them on an individual display for further manipulations.

- Object transfer: Moving an object from one display to another, such as moving an object to an individual workspace.

- Focusing-Brushing-Linking in collaborative MDEs: Focusing defines views on different displays that each convey only a subset of data. These views can be "linked" to the original data on the original display, so that any changes to the objects reflects simultaneously on the original display. Viewing a selected area on another display as a new workspace can be used for task distribution in a workshop scenario.

Furthermore, an extension to the within-display interaction primitive tasks is contributed as follows.

Visualization gallery: selecting objects for generating a new visualization of the data set or their metadata on the display (for example, geographical or statistical visualizations).

These cross-display interaction primitives are good bases for interaction designers, especially to design and evaluate a new input device for MDEs.

1.3.2 Practical Part

The second part of the research aimed to answer the following research questions, which the state-of-the-art techniques have left unanswered:

- **Does a mobile input device with an integrated display improve performing cross-display interaction tasks?**

    The idea behind this research was to compare two devices, one of which has an integrated display whereas the other does not. To answer the research question, a working prototype was implemented, called PrIME prototype, using a laser-pointing device and an iPhone as two alternative input devices for MDEs. A user study was conducted to compare these devices according to performance, as well as users' subjective feedback.

- **Using an iPhone as an input device to control a large display, which GUI and which ordering algorithm would be the fastest and the most preferable for the users?**

    Three different visualizations were implemented, namely CoverFlow, ZoomGrid and DisplayMap. For each of these visualizations, except for the DisplayMap, three different algorithms were used to put objects in order. Therefore, each user tested seven different conditions (DisplayMap + 3 * CoverFlow + 3* ZoomGrid). A user study was conducted to compare these 7 conditions.

- **What application domain can benefit from the PrIME prototype?**

    To show the application of the PrIME prototype concept in a real life scenario, CrossStorm prototype was implemented. CrossStorm supports users in brainstorming sessions for generating and posting post-its across displays.

1.4 Thesis Outline

This thesis is outlined as follows:

Related work

- Chapter 2 presents work related to this research in two categories. The first category highlights related research in the field of mobile devices as an input device. This section describes interesting research works that took advantage of the smart mobile devices to make a fluid interaction. The second category then, presents the research projects in the field of Multi-Display Environments (MDEs). These MDE methods are compared according to MDE requirements.

Theory

- Chapter 3 explains the background theory behind interaction with a single display as well as multiple displays. A list of primitive interaction tasks in MDEs are presented and illustrated as state transition networks.

Single-display interaction

- Chapter 4 highlights the experiences of designing, implementing, and evaluating a prototype in the ZKM — Center of Art and Media in Karlsruhe[1]. An iPhone in addition to an orientation sensor (InertiaCube sensor) was used as an input device to control a 360° panoramic display (PanoramaScreen at ZKM). The design challenges of the interaction concept are mentioned, and so are the solutions. The final section of this chapter describes the result of conducted user studies.

Methodology

- Chapter 5 explains the methodology behind this research. The steps taken to answer the research question are highlighted in the first part of this chapter. This is followed by a discussion on the potential input devices for MDEs together with their advantages and disadvantages. The third section then, explains the mechanism used to recognize the display on which the user was focusing via the Optitrack system. Finally, the last section of this chapter deals with the system infrastructure and architecture.

Multi-display interaction

- Chapter 6 highlights the lessons learned from the design and implementation of PrIME prototype, using a mobile input device with an integrated display for cross-display interaction selection and object-transfer tasks. Furthermore, this chapter describes the design and analysis of two user

---
[1] www.zkm.de

1.4 Thesis Outline

studies. The first experiment compared three potential GUIs for the iPhone, (namely, CoverFlow, DisplayMap, and ZoomGrid), whereas the second experiment compared two remote mobile devices, namely a laser-pointing device and an iPhone as representative devices without and with an integrated display.

- Chapter 7 points a few application domains, in which multiple displays can be beneficial. Additionally, a working prototype is introduced, which is based on the PrIME prototype. This prototype supports users in brainstorming sessions. In addition, the advantages and disadvantages of the system are discussed in this chapter.

  Application domain

- Chapter 8 sums up the thesis and lists the main achievements of this research. The possible extensions to the system and possible future work are mentioned in the last section.

  Conclusion

Chapter 2

Related work

> *"The only way to engineer the future tomorrow is to have lived in it yesterday."*
>
> — Bill Buxton, Sketching User Experiences, 2008

This research focuses on using mobile devices to control multiple displays. Therefore, two groups of research projects are considered as relevant, the first of which is the mobile device group, where mobile devices were used as an input device for controlling large displays. The second group consists of projects in multi-display environments, which did not necessarily use a mobile phone as an input device, but investigated interaction with multiple displays. This chapter, additionally investigates on existing object selection and object movement methods in multi-display environments.

2.1 Mobile Device Interaction

Weiser [1999] states that as Ubiquitous Computing (UbiComp) moves the computational resources beyond the desktop by blending them "into the fabric of our everyday lives", the need for novel interaction techniques is inevitable. People use computers not just at home or at the office, as in old days, but also in public areas such as bus stations, international exhibitions and airports. Traditional input devices, like the mouse and the keyboard, cannot be efficient for these post-desktop applications as in on-the-go scenarios the portability of the devices is necessary, as the user should be able to carry the device around [Jenabi, 2007].

In order to study these new existing challenges, researchers are designing and developing new devices. Different areas of applications have their own constraints, which need to be considered while designing new interaction techniques. As an example, in public areas, speech modality performs poorly because of the passengers' background noise. The question is whether one can develop standard equivalents to the traditional mouse and keyboard for UbiComp environments.

Mobile phones are some of the promising powerful devices that could be a good alternative for interaction in UbiComp environments. Mobile phones are the first truly pervasive computers that people use in everyday life. Some common activities which people regularly use their mobile for are calling friends, sending messages, Personal Information Management (PIM), or even playing games. Mobile phones are carried almost everywhere, all the time. They also have numerous built-in sensors such as cameras, accelerometer, touch display, and microphones. With such efficient features, mobile phones are powerful input devices that can be used to interact and control our environment [Haro et al., 2005].

These features make the mobile phone a good candidate as an input device; for example for controlling Large Public Displays (LPD). The number of LPDs is increasing in public places, such as airports, shopping malls, and bus stations, whereas the mouse and the keyboard are no longer proper input devices for such displays in ubiquitous computing environments, because this desktop metaphor restricts users' movements meanwhile interacting with a large display . Touch interaction is also not an option, since for LPDs the large size will make it difficult for the user to reach the display's upper corners. Using mobile phones in combination with LPDs can also improve the interaction in comparison with the mobile phone alone, since the small screen of the phone is not appropriate for high-resolution data representation.

Ballagas et al. [2005] have introduced the sweep technique that uses a mobile phone to control the cursor on an LPD (see

2.1 Mobile Device Interaction

figure 2.1 below). They use an optical flow algorithm that takes sequential pictures with the camera of a mobile phone, while the user is moving the phone in the air. The difference between the pictures enables them to compute the relative motion and map it to the cursor's relative movement on the display. With this technique the user can concentrate on his intended task with the LPD and does not need to look at the mobile phone during the interaction (eye-free interaction). With long-term usage, sweep can be a relatively high fatigue interaction, because of the arm movements [Ballagas, 2007].

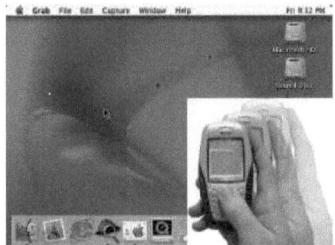

Figure 2.1: The sweep technique can be used to control a cursor on the large public display like an optical mouse [Ballagas, 2007].

Maunder et al. [2008] defined SnapAndGrab, which is an interaction technique using a mobile phone as an input device for interacting with an LPD. The user takes a picture from the media package of his interest, displayed on the LPD, and sends the picture to the SnapAndGrab display. The corresponding media object will then be sent back to the user using the Bluetooth connection. This interaction technique can be used select one item from a limited number of items (see figure 2.2 below).

Chan et al. [2005] presented a project with an orientation-aware handheld as an input device for a museum's application. Historical objects in the museum, which are located in front of the user, are shown on the handheld's display. As the user moves and turns, the view on the handheld display is updated to the current view in front of the device. The user can select an object of interest on his mobile phone by touching the screen and tapping on the object. Moreover, besides touching the display, body movement in this case is a way of interacting with the system (see figure 2.3 below).

Figure 2.2: The user is interested in item 'D' and takes a photo of it. The photo is sent to the SnapAndGrab display. Then, system sends back the media objects, via Bluetooth, that relate to media package 'D' [Maunder et al., 2008].

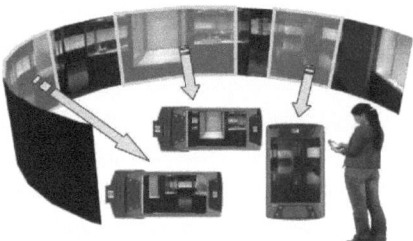

Figure 2.3: This figure illustrates an orientation-aware handheld, which is used as an input device in a museum [Chan et al., 2005].

In [Eissele et al., 2004] a prototype is implemented with a TabletPC in addition to an InertiaCube sensor that displays a virtual object at the same location and orientation as the real-world object. The user can explore the object from different views by moving the display around the object without any need to move the object itself.

Sanneblad and Holmquist [2006] have introduced a novel interaction technique using a mobile device in combination with a large display. The large display is responsible to show large images (context information). To view a detailed image of a

2.1 Mobile Device Interaction

special part, the user needs to hold a mobile device, such as a tablet PC, in front of an object of interest and the mobile device shows that part in a higher resolution (see figure 2.4 below).

Figure 2.4: The user holds up a tablet PC in front of a large projected image to view details [Sanneblad and Holmquist, 2006].

Boom Chameleon [Tsang et al., 2002] is a project that uses a handheld device as a "window to a virtual world". Without manipulating the physical artifact, the user can view its details by moving the handheld around the artifact (see figure 2.5 below).

Figure 2.5: The handheld device is used as a chameleon to view the details of the artifact (in this case, a car) without physically manipulating the artifact [Tsang et al., 2002].

ARC-Pad [McCallum and Irani, 2009] is a project that used a mobile phone with an integrated touch display to control a single large display. Users can use the touch screen of the mobile phone to move the mouse, by moving their finger to the left or right, up or down (relative pointing). Furthermore, users can perform an absolute pointing with the device by tapping with

ARC-Pad that causes the cursor to jump to the corresponding location on the screen, providing rapid movement across large distances. The mobile phone is connected to the display wirelessly. A comparison study showed that the ARC-Pad is faster than common relative pointing touch pads in performing target acquisition tasks on large displays.

Yang et al. [2010] have implemented the LenseMouse, which embeds a touch-screen display (HTC touch) to a normal mouse. The mouse is used for the usual relative pointing inside the display. The extra display attached to the mouse shows additional information, such as further navigation items, toolbars, palettes, pop-ups and other notification windows. This can save space on the desktop monitor, as well as shifting the annoying notifications of the system to the small display (see figure 2.6 below).

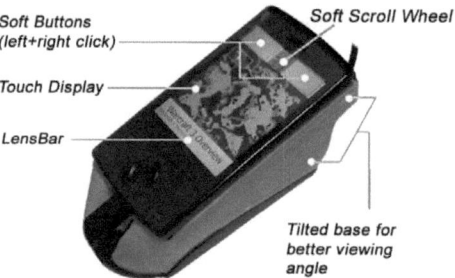

Figure 2.6: This figure shows the LensMouse, which is a novel input device with a normal mouse and an embedded touch screen [Yang et al., 2010].

2.2 Multi-Display Environments

There are many related works in the field of MDE that inspired this PhD research. Some early examples of such environments are iRoom at the Stanford University [Johanson et al., 2002] and i-Land [Streitz et al., 1999] at Fraunhofer IPSI [Prante et al., 2004].

The i-Land project used different interactive artifacts gathered

2.2 Multi-Display Environments

inside a smart room. The idea was to develop the workspace of the future to support meetings and brainstorming sessions. The room included a Dynawall, which is a vertical interactive display. It also included a CommChair, which is a chair that has an integrated TabletPC which is able to manipulate the objects on the DynaWall. A ConnecTable [Tandler, 2001] then, is an extension of the CommChair that allowed users to connect their TabletPCs together and move objects to another TabletPC. Transferring objects is also possible using a technique called Bridge technique. In this way, an object can be stored on a physical token and then transported to another display. The target display recognizes the token and presents the object stored on it.

Figure 2.7: This figure shows the i-Land environment. The user is annotating remotely from the CommChair to the DynaWall [Streitz et al., 1999].

As mentioned in [Nacenta et al., 2009], a fundamental between-display interaction is moving an object from one display to another. The Cristal project [Seifried et al., 2009] uses a touch table to control an interactive room. Simple touch gestures on the table can be used to transfer media data to a TV or even to turn on or turn off a lamp (see figure 2.8 below). Another project that also uses a touch table is WeSpace [Wigdor et al., 2009] (see figure 2.9 below), where a touch table is used to manage the view of different laptop screens on a large vertical display. The purpose of the system is to support presentations in a meeting room when researchers want to discuss their results.

Figure 2.8: This figure shows the setting for the Cristal project [Seifried et al., 2009]. The user is interacting with the analog display (the lamp) and digital display (the digital picture frame, TV) by using a touch table, which is located in front of him.

Figure 2.9: This figure shows the setting for the WeSpace project. [Wigdor et al., 2009]. Scientists connect their laptops with the large wall display, and can share their information and discuss about them in a group. Controlling the wall display is done by the touch table in front of the users.

IMPROMPTU [Biehl et al., 2008] introduced a framework for multi-display interaction, which also provides object movement, using mouse input. Documents that have to be discussed in a group can be transferred to a large display and users can set their data as sharable with others or have it kept privately (see figure 2.10 below). The framework was tested within two software development groups and this showed that the framework successfully supports information-sharing for collaborative work (see figure 2.11 below).

2.2 Multi-Display Environments

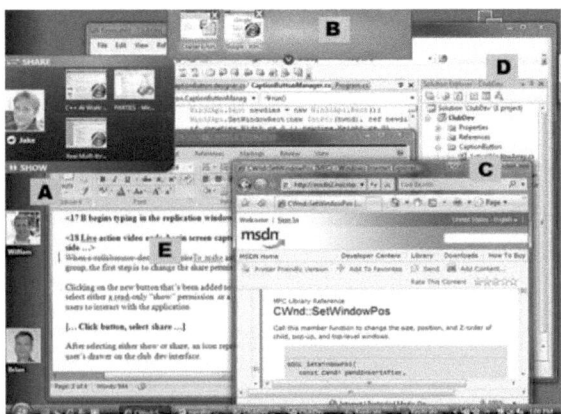

Figure 2.10: A screenshot of the IMPROMPTU user interface, along with replicated and local application windows on a user's machine. A collaborator bar is on the left (A), and one collaborator drawer is expanded showing the applications available to the group. The shared screen dock (B) allows windows to be placed on a large shared display. Whether an application is available to the group and what level of control is allowed can be set using (C). A replicated window in share mode allows interaction with its content (D); while a replicated window in show mode allows a user to view, but not to modify its content (E). [Biehl et al., 2008].

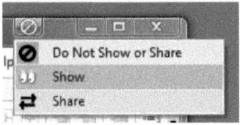

Figure 2.11: A screenshot of the privacy menu in IMPROMPTU [Biehl et al., 2008]. It is used to configure whether the window is available to the group, and whether group members can only view the application window (Show) or interact with it (Share).

Dynamo [Izadi et al., 2003] provides a large display that can be controlled with the mouse by multiple users. Each user has an individual part of the display, in order to browse the Internet or view multimedia data. Users are able to set security options, for instance, on who is allowed to edit their data (see figure2.12

below).

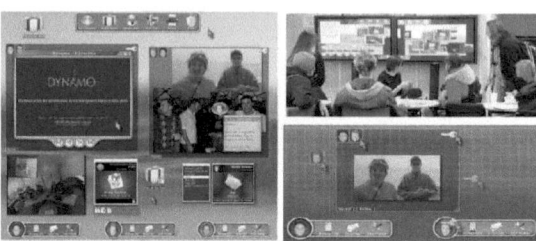

Figure 2.12: A screen shot of the Dynamo setting [Izadi et al., 2003]. It includes a selection of media, a public palette (located at the top of the display), personal palettes (located at bottom) and two carve regions

The Stitching technique [Hinckley et al., 2004] allows the sharing of objects from one display to another. It detects the relationship between pen strokes that are performed across the two displays, which can be located directly next to each other or even at a distance (see figure 2.13 below).

Figure 2.13: This figure illustrates the stitching technique for moving an object from one display to another [Hinckley et al., 2004].

In addition to the object movement interaction, related works have investigated other applicable prototypes taking advantage of multiple displays. Forlines et al. [2006] use a touch table and/or a tablet PC for controlling a multi-display setting. They also show different views of Google Earth on different displays (3 wall displays, one touch table, and a tablet PC). On one display users can see a 3D building visualization on the Google application. Simultaneously a visualization of streets and schools located in that area is displayed on the other vertical displays. Users interact with the geographical interface using their tablet

2.2 Multi-Display Environments

PC or touch table. Users can use their own tablet PC to work privately on the visualization, and not to disturb their colleagues. To increase awareness concerning teamwork, people can use the touch table to interact. This research is an example of how multiple displays can be used for showing different, but synchronized views (see figure 2.14 below).

Another authentic example of such a scenario is the Deskotheque [Pirchheim et al., 2009] project. It uses the Caleydo application [Streit et al., 2009], a Visual Analysis Framework for Gene Expression Data, in the context of biology, in order to view various synchronized biomedical visualizations in parallel on multiple displays. In this domain, having different biomedical visualizations can help study the interdependencies of the gene products (see figure 2.15 below).

Figure 2.14: Two users working with the multi-device, multi-user adaptation of Google Earth [Forlines et al., 2006]. A touch table in front of the users is used to control the views on other dislays.

TouchProjector [Boring et al., 2010] is a project that uses video streaming data, which is taken by an iPhone camera to manipulate objects. An iPhone can also transfer an object from one display to another, even remotely (see figure 2.17 below). Several other researchers have investigated using hand-held devices for controlling their environment. For example, Pebbles project [1] uses PDAs as a universal controller. Semantic Snarfing [Myers et al., 2001] is a method used to indicate the region of interest on the display using a laser pointer or fingeror eye tracking. This information is then copied to the screen of a handheld device.

---

[1] http://www.pebbles.hcii.cmu.edu/puc

Figure 2.15: Deskotheque setup with multiple projections and personal workspaces [Pirchheim et al., 2009].

Figure 2.16: Deskotheque using Caleydo application [Streit et al., 2009].

Slay and Thomas [2006] implemented a UIC (universal interaction controller). UIC is an input device designed for interacting with multiple displays in a ubiquitous environment. The device ca be used to select, copy and paste objects. The researchers' aim was to determine the intuitiveness of their universal interaction controller input device in order to support the interaction and control of the data displayed on heterogeneous devices simultaneously in a multi-display environment. They ran a user study to compare the performance of operating with a wireless gyroscopic mouse and a UIC (universal interaction controller), benchmarked with the performance using a traditional mouse. The result showed that after an hour of training users had a better performance using the UIC rather than the traditional mouse. UIC performed better than the wireless gyroscopic mouse even without training (see figure 2.18 below).

2.2 Multi-Display Environments

Figure 2.17: A screen shot of the TouchProjector project [Boring et al., 2010] that uses an Apple iPhone to interact with multiple displays. The system is based on a video-stream analysis. The videos are taken from the camera of the iPhone.

Figure 2.18: The user is interacting across displays with UIC [Slay and Thomas, 2006]. In such situations, users can point to an object to select it and then use his/her stylus to perform fine grained manipulation.

G–stalt [Zigelbaum et al., 2010] is a project based on g-speak platform of oblong industries [2]. Users wear hand gloves and apply hand gestures, in order to navigate the media data on the display, as well as to transfer one object from a large vertical

---
[2]http://oblong.com/

projected display to a table top. The data presentation and manipulation is done in 3 dimensions. The advantage of the system is direct interaction with the objects. The researchers demonstrated the system on different events and found that the used gesture set was complicated for users. A disadvantage of this system is that users need to memorize the gestures and they also do not have any visible controls.

Figure 2.19: A screen shot of the G-stalt project [Zigelbaum et al., 2010].

In the following section some of the requirements for MDEs are presented and discussed according to the above-mentioned projects.

2.3 MDE Requirements

The following characteristics are necessary for co-located collaboration in MDEs. Each of the requirements are explained and different examples from the above-mentioned related work are mentioned.

Bi-directional Interaction
In order to support an equal participation in collaboration, all the users need to be given an opportunity to transfer objects from any display to any other display. Therefore, regardless of touch-sensitiveness and other specific features, displays should be controllable bi-directionally. The Cristal project [Seifried et al., 2009] is a useful setting as a home application, when people want to control the devices in the room. However, if one wants to extend the system for collaborative work scenarios,

2.3 MDE Requirements

this uni-directional control may not allow users at any display to control and manipulate the objects. WeSpace [Wigdor et al., 2009] is also implemented for presentations in a meeting room, when researchers want to discuss their results. A touch table is a potential control device in this setting, but in a workshop scenario, where people are divided into sub groups and each sub group collaborates separately in parallel, a bi-directional control is more adequate. This problem is solved in Stitching [Hinckley et al., 2004], since any object can be transferred to another display using a pen.

Privacy & Awareness
Another important issue in collaboration scenarios is awareness. Cristal [Seifried et al., 2009] and WeSpace [Wigdor et al., 2009] increase the level of group awareness by using a touch table, which may not always be desirable in collaborative work. For instance, when users want to enter a keyword for searching, publicly presenting the keyword on the table might be undesirable. Hand-held devices in such settings increase the users' privacy, as tablet PC is used in [Forlines et al., 2006].

Another aspect of privacy is the possibility to configure which information is sharable with others and which should be kept private. This feature exists in Dynamo [Izadi et al., 2003] and IMPROMPTU [Biehl et al., 2008].

Mobility
Mobility is a necessary feature in ubiquitous computing environments, especially in collaborative spaces where people are free to change their position or perspective while performing joint tasks [Ha et al., 2006]. Users should be able to move around and interact with the surrounding displays. Systems that use a touch table or a mouse to control the displays encounter this problem. Such systems include Cristal [Seifried et al., 2009], WeSpace [Wigdor et al., 2009], IMPROMPTU [Biehl et al., 2008] and Dynamo [Izadi et al., 2003]. Systems that use mobile input devices, such as PDAs, mobile phones, or laser pointers (e.g. TouchProjector [Boring et al., 2010], a tablet PC [Forlines et al., 2006]) offer a solution to this problem.

Reachability & Flexibility
Some of the related works present novel solutions for MDEs based on specific features of the displays (e.g., touch sensitiveness). Therefore generalizing the solution for any kind

of display is not always straightforward. For instance, the object transfer technique in Stitching [Hinckley et al., 2004] is applicable only for pen-based displays, which are not flexible enough to interact with different kinds of displays. Furthermore, this technique cannot be used if the displays are not reachable due to, for example, a crowd of people in a presentation session. TouchProjector [Boring et al., 2010] solves this problem by using a mobile phone to transfer the objects.

Generalization of Single-Purpose Applications
State-of-the-art techniques in cross-display interaction have investigated different prototypes to transfer objects or to distribute different visualizations on displays. Lessons learned from these single-purpose solutions can help in the design of future MDE applications. For example, Deskotheque [Pirchheim et al., 2009] and Forlines et al. [2006] have shown that enabling users to actively manage visualizations on different displays enhances collaborative work and should be generalized and integrated into cross-display interaction. However, a number of disadvantages of current systems are recognized, namely uni-directional control, the provision of a stationary controlling mechanism that hinders the freedom of movement in the room, privacy and awareness issues, as well as flexibility of the interaction regardless of specific features of the display (e.g., pen-based or touch-sensitive).

Comparison Between the Methods
In the previous section, the requirements of the MDEs were listed and for each example , some research works were mentioned. In the table 2.1, the research works are compared according to the MDE requirements. The privacy of the projects is compared in two columns. The interaction privacy refers to whether the observers can recognize the user's actions. The privacy of information refers to whether the system allows the user to set their data to "just viewable", "editable", and so on.

2.4 Object Selection and Movement Methods in MDEs

This section gives an overview of relevant existing methods used for object selection and object movements across displays. Not

2.4 Object Selection and Movement Methods in MDEs

Related Works	Bi-directional Control	Mobility	Reachability & Flexibility	Awareness	Interaction Privacy	Information Privacy
WeSpace	-	-	+	+	-	-
Cristal	-	-	+	+	-	-
TouchProjector	+	+	+	-	+	-
Deskotheque	-	-	+	+	-	-
Forline et al.	-	-	+	+	mixed	-
Impromptu	+	-	+	+	-	+
Stitching	+	+	-	+	-	-
G-stalt	+	+	+	+	-	-
Dynamo	-	-	+	+	-	+
iLand	+	+	-	mixed	mixed	-

Table 2.1: This table compares the related works according to the MDE requirements criteria. The sign -, shows that the system lacks this requirement, + shows that the system fulfills the requirements whereas mixed, means that some devices used in the system lack the requirement whereas some fulfill it. For example, the prototype of Forline and his colleagues uses a touch table which fulfills the awareness requirement, but not the interaction privacy. This system has the possibility to use a Tablet PC as well, which lacks the awareness criterion, but fulfills the interaction privacy issue.

all the methods for object selection and movement are presented here, but only the ones that are suitable for collaborative environments with combination of shared and private displays.

2.4.1 Slingshot

As the name implies, Slingshot [Hascoët, 2003] is a technique that works like a slingshot. The user touches an object with a digital Pen, moves it backwards and finally releases it. The object moves forward proportional to the size of the pen's backward stoke (see figure 2.20 below).

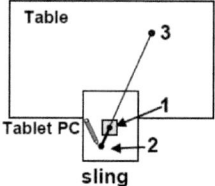

Figure 2.20: Slingshot and Pantograph. 1 is the initial position of the pen, 2 is the current position of the pen, and 3 is the destination of the object (reference: [Hascoët, 2003]).

2.4.2 Pick and Drop

This method was designed by Rekimoto [1997]. An object can be selected using a digital stylus from a tabletPC. User taps on an object using a stylus. Then he/she lifts the stylus and move it to another display. As the stylus touches another display, the object is placed in that position. This method is direct, and cannot be done remotely. Another drawback of this method is that it just works with the stylus (see figure 2.21 below).

2.4.3 Hyperdragging

This method is also suggested by Rekimoto and Saitoh [1999]. As a user put his or her laptop on the table (see figure 2.23 below), a

2.4 Object Selection and Movement Methods in MDEs 27

Figure 2.21: This figure illustrates the Pick and Drop method using a digital stylus. User picks an object with a pen by taping on it and move it to another display. Hitting the new display transfers the object to that point (reference: [Rekimoto, 1997]).

camera, which is installed above the table, recognizes the marker attached to the laptop and detects who the device belongs to, as well as the location of the device. When the user drags an object to the edge of the screen with a mouse, the object is transferred to the VCR tape on the table as a voice record (see figure 2.22 below). This spatially continuous workspace is getting closer to the object movements in the physical world.

2.4.4 Lift and Drop

Lift and Drop is another method presented by Bader et al. [2010]. This method is based on Airlift, which is a video-based input that can track the user's hand and fingertips' positions' independent of the display. This information is used for the interaction, which allows a consistent interaction across display boundaries (see figure 2.24 below). Lift and Drop is a direct technique that is similar to the Pick and Drop, and can copy an object from one display to another, but additionally presents the movement feedback on the display. A user study, which was done by Bader et al. [2010], showed that the continuous feedback of the Lift and Drop technique slows down the user's interaction in comparison to the Pick and Drop. Regardless of this, after training the interaction speed stays in the same level for both techniques. Moreover, user satisfaction was higher for the Lift and Drop technique.

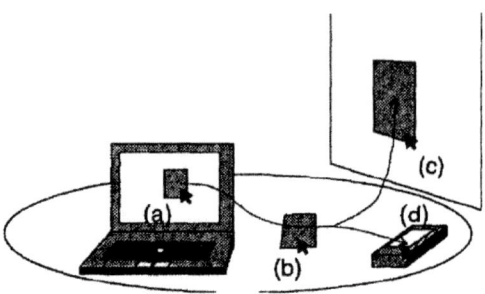

Figure 2.22: Hyperdragging: A spatially continuous interaction technique for moving information between computers. (a) A user can start moving an object on a computer in the usual way, that is, by dragging it with the pointing device (b) When the cursor reaches the edge of the screen, it "jumps" to the table surface. (c) The user can continue to drag it to another surface, such as a wall. (d) The user can also drop an item on a physical object, such as a VCR tape, to link real and virtual objects [Rekimoto and Saitoh, 1999].

Figure 2.23: As a user puts his or her laptop on the table, a camera, which is installed above the table, recognizes the marker attached to the laptop and detect to whom the device belongs, as well as the location of the device [Rekimoto and Saitoh, 1999].

2.4 Object Selection and Movement Methods in MDEs

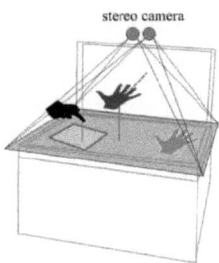

Figure 2.24: This figure pictures the Lift and Drop technique suggested by Bader et al. [2010]. Input by multiple users can be recognized, independent from the display they want to control. The user's hand and finger inputs are recognized by a camera.

2.4.5 Drag and Pop

Drag-and-pop [Baudisch et al., 2003] is an extension of the Drag and Drop method, which is known from traditional desktop interfaces. This method is designed for interacting with displays using touch or a pen. When a display is at a distance, it may be difficult to access the data. This technique helps by "popping up" the related objects and placing them temporarily close to the cursor, so that the user can reach them with small hand movements. For example, when a user wants to delete an item (see figure 2.25 below), s/he drags the item toward the recycle bin. As the user moves the pointer, the Drag and Pop pops up similar objects of the same type that are located in the same direction.

2.4.6 Drag and Pick

Drag and Pick is another method which was also designed by Baudisch et al. [2003]. Its purpose was to support access to the content on displays at a distance. It differs from the Drag and Pop method in two ways. First, as the user starts dragging an object, not just the objects with compatible type, but all the objects in the direction of the mouse movement are activated. Secondly, as the user drags the mouse to a target item and releases it, the

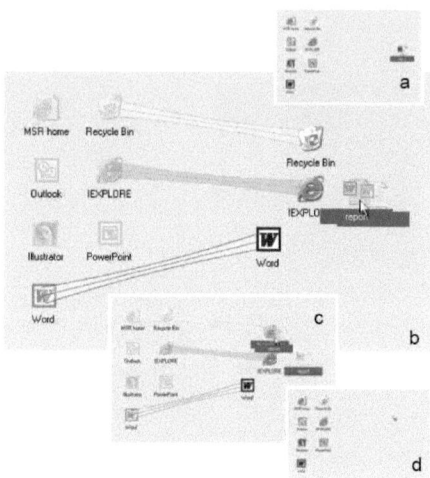

Figure 2.25: Drag and Pop is an easier method used for accessing an object or content of information on large displays. This technique helps by "popping up" the related objects and placing them temporarily close to the cursor.(a) The user intends to delete a Word memo by dragging it into the recycle bin. (b) As the user starts dragging the memo's icon towards the recycle bin, icons that are of compatible type and located in the direction of the user's drag motion "pop up". This means that for each of these icons a link icon is created (tip icon) that appears in front of the user's cursor. Tip icons are connected to the original icon (base icon) using a rubber band. (c) The user drags the memo over the recycle bin and releases the mouse button. The recycle bin accepts the memo. Alternatively, the user could have dropped the memo over the word processor or the web browser icon, which would have launched the respective application with the memo. (d) When the user drops the icon, all tip icons disappear instantly.[Baudisch et al., 2003].

application, file or folder associated with that icon is opened, as if it has been double-clicked (see figure 2.26 below).

A comparison between the Pick and Drop and Slingshot methods is done by Nacenta et al. [2005]. The result showed that Pick and Drop works better than the Slingshot. Researchers concluded that it is more efficient to offer the users local feedback than feedback at the distant target.

Figure 2.26: Drag-and-pick allows users to temporarily move icons from an external monitor to the tablet where the user can interact with them using a pen [Baudisch et al., 2003].

2.5 Summary of the Chapter

This chapter presented work related to this research in two categories. The first category highlighted related research in the field of mobile devices as an input device. The interesting research work, described in this section, took advantage of the smart mobile devices to make a fluid interaction. The second category then, includes the research projects in the field of MDEs. These MDE methods were compared to each other according to MDE requirements. Such requirements should be considered for prototyping new interaction techniques in MDEs.

Chapter 3

Theory

"It is the theory that decides what can be observed."
—Albert Einstein

This chapter explains the theory behind the interaction tasks in single and multiple display environments. The following section defines what displays are.

3.1 Displays

A display is defined as a collection of individually controllable pixels [Chandler et al., 2009]. In a traditional display, the pixels are arranged in fixed two dimensional grid. An infrastructure is provided to control the pixels in real time. Newer technologies, such as emergent displays allow for decentralized approach, where each pixel is considered as an intelligent, self-organizing computational device, interconnected to the others through a loosely coupled communication network. Firefly prototype is based on this technology, which is explained in [Chandler et al., 2009].

Displays can be of different sizes and with different functions, such as touch sensitive. Mobile devices, such as mobile phones, PDAs, TabletPCs, and laptops, have their own integrated display. Public environments, such as airports and train stations, include large displays for presenting advertisement or information about time schedules. Most of these displays are usually not interactive. Nowadays, the number of interactive displays are increasing in such environments. Furthermore, meeting rooms, discussion rooms and workshops with collaborative groups have started using multiple displays, such as for the viewing of different visualization of data for comparison and cooperation, (for example, for biochemists, designers, engineers, architects). Multiple displays can solve occlusion problems that exists in a single display using several windows. Additionally, it supports the cognitive partitioning of the information.

Several research works investigate interacting with single and multiple displays using different types of input devices. Some researchers attempted to make a formal presentation of the interaction with input devices by listing the tasks or making classifications and taxonomies. The following section presents the result of such researches for interacting with a single display.

3.2 Single-Display Interaction

"The entry of each symbol by the user is an interaction task, performed by means of an interaction technique. Each task can be implemented by many different techniques. The designers of the system must select interaction techniques that best match both the user's characteristics and the specific requirements of the task, and they must also select the appropriate device." [Foley et al., 1984]

The following sections introduce researchers' earlier attempts to define a list of basic interaction tasks for single-display environments.

3.2.1 Primitive Interaction Tasks for Single-Display Environments

Primitive interaction tasks for single-display environments

Foley et al. [1984] defined the *interaction tasks* as primitive nonterminal symbols, several of which form a command to an interactive system. The researchers mention a "move entity"

3.2 Single-Display Interaction

command as an example with three such symbols, namely a position, an entity, and the imperative move. An interaction task is a user's entry of each symbol, which is performed by means of an *interaction technique*. The designers' role is to select a proper interaction technique that matches both the user's characteristics as well as the task requirements. On the other hand, the designer should select a proper input device.

Foley et al. suggested that there are six fundamental types of interaction tasks. These tasks are independent of application and hardware and act as building blocks of more complex interaction tasks that then form a complete interaction dialogue. The list of tasks is user-oriented, which means that it presents the units of a user's actions. These tasks are as follows.

- **Select**: it means that a user makes a selection from a set of alternatives. Some possible interaction techniques are menu selection using a mouse, typing in a name, abbreviation or number on a keyboard or voice input.
- **Position**: when a user indicates a position on a display. Possible interaction techniques are through the use of a mouse, or typing in a coordination.
- **Orient**: as the name implies, it aims at orienting an entity in 2-D or 3-D, such as rotating an image. Examples of interaction techniques are rotating using a mouse, or entering angle degrees using a keyboard.
- **Path**: users generate this task by a series of positions and orientations over the time. Digitalizing a sketch or showing a route on a map are some examples of path.
- **Quantity**: specifying a value to quantify a measure, such as the height of an entity. Interaction techniques, such as typing-in on a keyboard or moving a slider to set the value, fall under this category.
- **Text**: it consists of entering a text string such as an annotation. Typing-in on a keyboard or selecting characters from an on-display menu are some examples of interaction techniques.

Interaction tasks

The above-mentioned tasks do not modify an object. For this to happen, a user must first select the object and then manipulate that object using a special program. Modification is an example of a task that attempts to control an object. These tasks, which Foley et al. [1984] have called *controlling tasks*, are also elementary since they are not achievable through a sequence of other elementary tasks. The list of controlling tasks are highlighted below.

Controlling tasks

- **Stretch**: it starts as a user grasps a feature and moves to a new position, leaving the other features of the object in place. Typical stretching techniques are stretched lines or vertices.

- **Sketch**: it is performed by manipulating a locating device which creates an object by freehand sketching. Sketching is the controlling version of the path.

- **Manipulate**: it includes moving an object by translation or orientation, as well as scaling. Some manipulation techniques are dragging and twisting.

- **Shape**: it is performed when a user causes a smooth, curved line or surface to change its general shape according to the placement of a positioning device.

Hinckley [2007] argued that the above list has to be extended, since newer technology, such as global positioning system (GPS) readers, cameras, and fingerprint scanners do not fit in this list. For example, in the case of fingerprint scanners, authentication can be suggested as an elementary task. Buxton [1986] mentioned another drawback of the list, namely that it does not define the level of analysis for the elementary tasks. For instance, a mouse indicates an (x, y) position, but another device, such as a Etch-a-Sketch, provides one knob for x and another knob for y. Therefore, this would divide the position task to two sub-tasks, (see figure 3.1 below). In order to solve this problem, Buxton [1986] suggested a hierarchical view of tasks to sub-tasks. In this way, a task is elementary or does not depend on the input device used for the task.

Although Hinckley [2007] and Buxton [1986] argued that device-specific capabilities can influence the tasks that users can perform, hardware- and software-specific issues are beyond the scope of this research work, which aims at extending Foley's approach for multi-display environments. Therefore, this

3.2 Single-Display Interaction

ISO's Task Primitives	Foley	Comments
Code Input	Text	The same for both groups
Pointing	Point	The same for both groups
Dragging	Drag	Foley considered Drag as a controlling task.
Selecting	Select	The same for both groups
Tracing	Point + Path	Combining pointing with the path in Foley's list can generate tracing task

Table 3.1: This table lists the task primitives for single displays according to the ISO 9241-400 in the first column. The second column presents the similar task according to the Foley's list. The third column provides some comments about this comparison.

research only consider device-independent and user-centered interaction tasks.

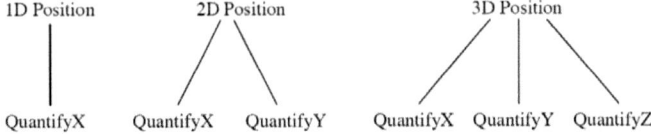

Figure 3.1: This figure portrays the task hierarchies for 1D, 2D, and 3D position tasks (reference: [Hinckley, 2007]).

3.2.2 ISO 9241-400 List of Primitive Tasks

ISO standard in "ergonomics of human system interaction-physical input devices-ergonomic principles" lists the primitive interaction tasks for single-display environment as can be seen in table 3.1, first column. These tasks are all included in the list of Foley et al. [1984], where dragging, however, was considered as a controlling task.

For a multi-display environment, such a list has not been investigated in the literature as yet. The following section highlights the primitive tasks in these environments.

3.3 Multi-Display Interaction

Primitive interaction tasks for MDEs (PrIME) are a subset of all the interaction tasks for MDEs. The main characteristic of the PrIME is that all the interaction tasks can be formed using a sequence of primitive interaction tasks for single displays and/or primitive interaction tasks for multiple displays. The presented list in this research work is an attempt to achieve this aim and is not guaranteed to be complete. As research in this field makes progress, more primitive tasks might need to be added. The set of interaction tasks is illustrated in figure 3.2 below. The contribution of this research is to list the interaction tasks in area D. The relationship between the subsets are as follows.

$C =$ Primitive tasks for within-display interaction
$D - C =$ Primitive tasks for between-display interaction
$B \cup D \subset A$
$B \cap D = C$

Boundaries of PrIME set

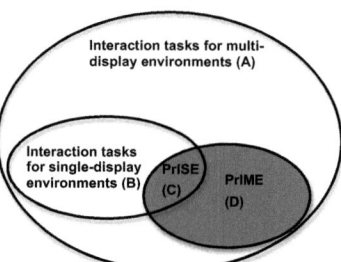

Figure 3.2: This figure illustrates the boundaries of the PrIME set. Area A shows the set of interaction tasks for multi-display environments. This area includes area B, which in turn includes all the interaction tasks for single-display environments. Additionally, this area also includes area C, which is the set of PrISE (primitive interaction tasks for single-display environment). Area D then, presents the set of PrIME (primitive interaction tasks for multi-display environment). The PrISE set has already been investigated by other researchers, (refer to section 3.2). The contribution of this research is to add one primitive task to area C and to define three primitive tasks for area D.

3.3 Multi-Display Interaction

These tasks are inspired by example applications, mentioned earlier in chapter 2. The possible interaction tasks for each example application are studied and respectively, the primitives are added to the list. As mentioned earlier, the list is application- and hardware-independent.

The primitive tasks for multi-display environments, that extend the primitive tasks for single-display interaction, are mentioned below.

- **Object selection**: selecting one or more objects from one or more displays, for example, to collect objects of interest from different displays and drop them on an individual display for further manipulations (extension of selection in single-display interaction by Foley et al. [1984]).
- **Object transfer**: moving one or more objects from one or more displays to another, such as moving an object to an individual workspace (inspired by [Hinckley et al., 2004], etc.).
- **Focusing-Brushing-Linking in collaborative MDEs**: focusing defines views on different display each of which convey only a subset of data. These views can be "linked" to the original data on the original display, so that any changes to the objects reflect simultaneously on the original display. Viewing a selected area on another display as a new workspace, can be used for task distribution in a workshop scenario (inspired by [Forlines et al., 2006], [Isenberg and Fisher, 2009], [Pirchheim et al., 2009]).

An extension to the within-display interaction primitives is as follow.

- **Visualization gallery**: selecting objects to generate a new visualization of the data set or their metadata on the display (for example, geographical or statistical visualizations); (inspired by [Streit et al., 2009]).

These cross-display interaction primitives are good bases for interaction designers, especially to design and evaluate a new input device for MDEs.

3.3.1 Object Selection

Before performing any of the next primitive tasks, users must select the objects of their interest. Object selection is already considered as a single-display primitive task (in ISO 9241-400 and [Foley et al., 1984]). However, it has to be considered as a primitive task in cross-display interaction as well, since users may want to select different objects from different displays.

There are different interaction techniques that can be used to select an object in an MDE. A few are mentioned below.

- Selecting by menu navigation

- Selecting by view and tap (using a mouse, a laser-pointing device or an iPhone)

- Selecting by searching keywords

- Selecting by voice: saying the name of the object.

Figure 3.3: This mockup illustrates an interaction technique used to select an abstract object using an iPhone. This technique is also used in PrIME prototype, which is explained in chapter 6.

In the PrIME prototype, which is presented in chapter 6, the interaction technique used to select objects is by view and tap. Users can see the objects on an iPhone as a CoverFlow visualization and can select them by tapping with a finger (see figure 3.3 above).

3.3 Multi-Display Interaction

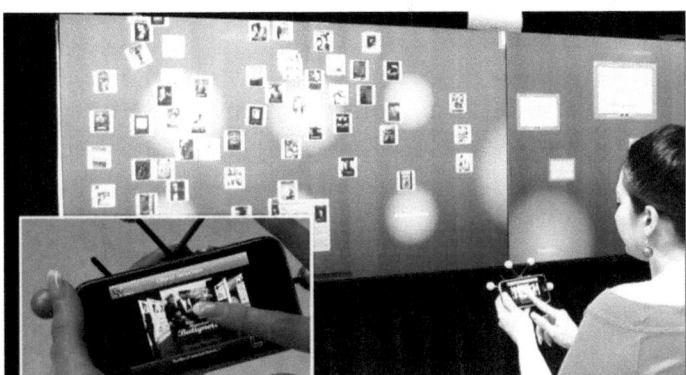

Figure 3.4: This mockup illustrates an interaction technique used to select an object with an iPhone. This technique is also used in PrIME prototype, which is explained in chapter 6.

Figure 3.5: This mockup illustrates an interaction technique where objects are selected using a laser-pointing device. This technique is explained in chapter 6.

3.3.2 Object Transfer

Users can move one object from one display to another. Nacenta et al. [2009] specifies the cross-display object movement, (the action of moving a cursor or digital object from a specific location in one display to a specific location in another display), as one of the core functionalities that allow fluid interaction in MDEs.

Different interaction techniques can be applied to move objects across displays. In the following list, some techniques are highlighted.

- Transferring objects using a digital pen, (for example, in Stitching technique [Hinckley et al., 2004])
- Transferring objects by using gestures in the air, (for example, in the G-stalt project [Zigelbaum et al., 2010])
- Transferring objects using a laser-pointing device, (This research includes the implementation of this method. This technique is explained in further detail in chapter 6.)
- Transferring objects using an input device with an integrated display. The display can be used as a clipboard while the user is moving an object from one display to another, as can be seen in figure 3.6 below. (This method is also implemented in PrIME prototype, which is mentioned in chapter 6).

3.3.3 Focusing-Brushing-Linking in Collaborative MDEs

Keim [2002] explains the linking and brushing as follows.

"The idea of linking and brushing is to combine different visualization methods to overcome the shortcomings of single techniques. Interactive changes made in one visualization are automatically reflected in the other visualizations. Note that connecting multiple visualizations through interactive linking and brushing provides more information than considering the component visualizations independently."

3.3 Multi-Display Interaction

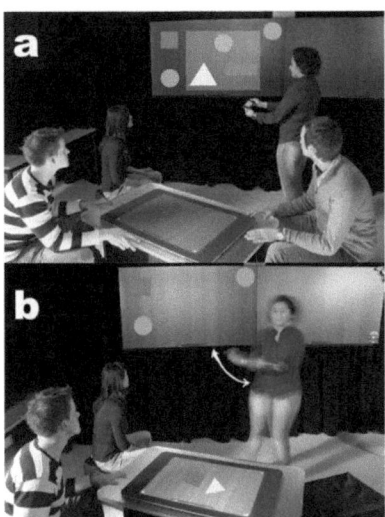
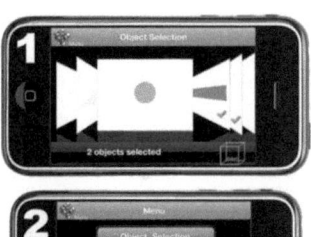

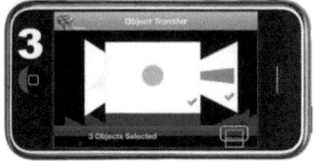

Figure 3.6: This mockup illustrates an interaction technique used to transfer objects from one display to another using an iPhone. This technique is also used in PrIME prototype, which is explained in chapter 6. The user can view the objects on the display as a cover flow visualization on the iPhone (figure 1). Selecting objects is done by tapping with a finger. The user turns to the target display and can move the objects to that display by selecting "object transfer" from the menu in figure 2. The iPhone is as a clipboard, that shows the current selected objects as the user moves around with the device (figure 3).

Voigt [2002] adds to this by stating.

"Brushing means selecting a subset of the data items with an input device (mouse). This is usually done to highlight this subset, but it can also be done to delete it from the view or to de-emphasize it, if the user wants to focus on the other items. Brushing is most interesting in connection with linking. For instance in a scatterplot matrix, the user could brush some points in one plot. This causes the brush effect (highlighting, etc.) to be applied on those points in the other plots that represent the same data items."

Furthermore, Buja et al. [1991] clarifies the advantages of focusing by saying that "it is usually more effective to construct a number of simple, easy to understand displays, each focused clearly on a particular aspect of the underlying data."

The focus of this work is on focusing, brushing and linking, only in multi-display environments, where a subset of data can be focused on an extra display. For instance, in teamwork scenarios, it is necessary to define individual or subgroup workspaces, such as, in the case of different groups working simultaneously on different objects using different displays. Therefore, each display focuses on a part of information, but any changes to that subset of information, simultaneously makes changes on the original display. It may only be necessary to define not only the workspace management, but also different views or windows over a sub-collection of objects, in general, for instance, to present different perspectives of a topic using different sets of data.

The difference between defining a view and transferring objects is that when views are defined on the information landscape, manipulations on the objects are synchronized among all the displays that have defined this object as part of their view. This helps when people want to synchronize their work on a specific object. In comparison, object transfer includes simply transferring an object to another display. Further manipulations to that object are only possible on that specific display, without any synchronization. One can simplify these two interaction types and define them as: object transfer = paste as independent objects, and view management = paste as linked objects.

Some applications of focusing and linking occur in the fields of linguistics, geographic information systems, time series analysis, and the analysis of multi-channel images arising in radiology and remote sensing [Buja et al., 1991].

Different interaction techniques can be used to perform the focusing, brushing and linking task. One example is illustrated in figure 3.7 below, where an iPhone is used to select a subset of objects on the vertical display, and transfer them to the horizontal display (Microsoft Surface) as linked objects.

Isenberg and Fisher [2009] extended the traditional brushing and linking technique and defines *collaborative brushing and linking* as follows.

3.3 Multi-Display Interaction

"An awareness technique, in which the interactions of one collaborator on a visualization are visible to other collaborators viewing the data items in their own visualizations or views of the data."

This concept adds information to the social data analysis process and it is also applicable to multi-display environments, where users are collaborating using shared and individual displays simultaneously. Therefore, inspired by this definition, in this research the task of focusing-brushing-linking is called focusing-brushing-linking in collaborative MDEs. The interesting point is that the three concepts of multi-view, multi-display and multi-user are combined together in the concept of co-located collaborative work.

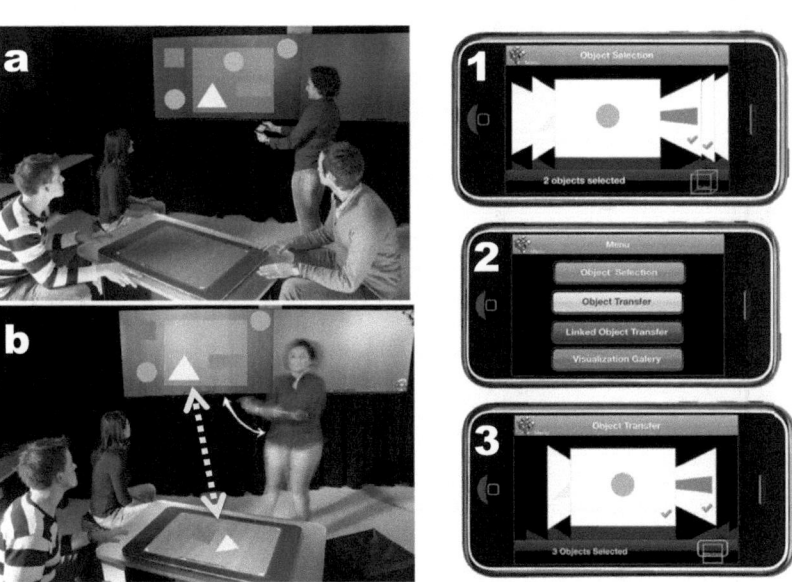

Figure 3.7: This mockup illustrates an interaction technique where objects are being transferred from one display to another by keeping a link to the original display using an iPhone. Any changes on the objects on the target display (Microsoft Surface) will change the original objects on the Cube display as well.

3.3.4 Visualization Gallery

In business group discussions, multiple visualizations may be necessary for presentation issues, or to compare different results. This different visualization can be a simple visualization of the selected images on a small screen in a bigger size on another display (as also used in Stitching [Hinckley et al., 2004]). The visualization could get more complex by showing different diagrams of the same dataset on different displays (for example, scatter plot, grid, or locations on Google Maps). In multi-display settings one can use an input device with an integrated display, such as an iPhone, to manage and select the desired visualization. This interaction type can be simplified to paste as a new visualization.

Figure 3.8: This mockup illustrates an interaction technique for visualization gallery using an iPhone.

This research defines visualization gallery as a primitive interaction task for single-display environments (PrISE), since this tasks is also possible with only one display. Therefore, the visualization gallery for a multi-display environment can be generated as:

Visualization Gallery for MDE = object selection for MDE + linking the displays for MDE + visualization Gallery for single display interaction

In this section, the primitive interaction tasks for multi-display environments are listed. These tasks are illustrated in area D in figure 3.2 above. One example for area A would be, when a user configures multiple displays simultaneously, such as, when the user makes all the displays brighter. This interaction task can be defined by two primitive tasks in the abstract level, namely linking the brightness feature of the displays together as a primitive task of a multi-display environment, and manipulating the brightness which is included in the primitive task for single display interaction (manipulation + linking).

3.4 PrIME Diagrammatic Notations

In this section, state transition networks (STN) of the primitive interaction tasks in MDE are presented. Before presenting these, the STN is described.

3.4.1 State Transition Networks

State transition networks have been used for a long time to describe dialogues [Dix et al., 2004]. Circles present a state, and the lines between the states are the transitions from one state to another. The text above the line shows the action, which is performed by a user whereas the text below the line shows the system's reactions or feedbacks. Figure 3.9 below shows a state transition network of a drawing software, where a user can select either a circle or a line from a menu. By selecting the circle button,

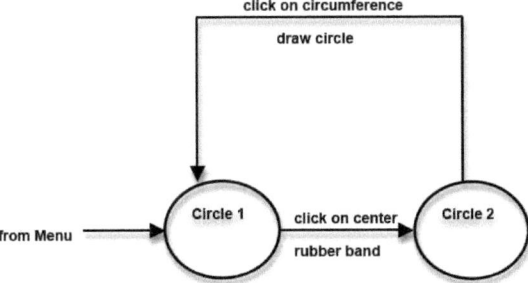

Figure 3.9: This figure shows an example of a state transition diagram for a drawing tool (reference: [Dix et al., 2004]).

two clicks are enough to draw a circle. The two clicks specify the circle and a point on the circumference of the circle. For systems with more functionalities the STN may become complex and less readable. Therefore another extension of the STNs that are called Hierarchical STNs can be used. Hierarchical STNs include rectangles in addition to the STN notation. Each rectangle represents an STN. In the software application mentioned above, in addition to drawing, one can add text to each drawing created, as well as select the freehand paint option to be able to draw with a brush. The hierarchical STN notation of this example is illustrated in figure 3.10 below.

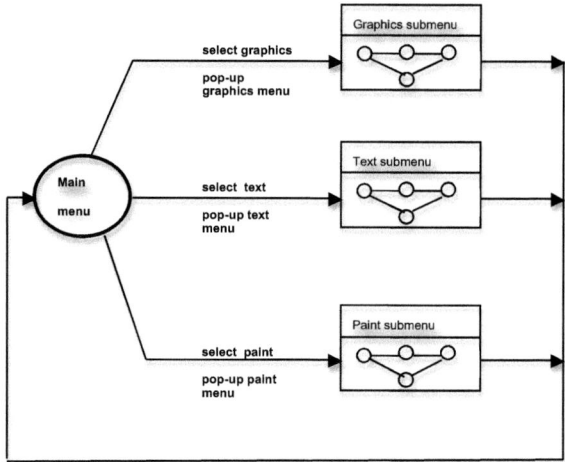

Figure 3.10: This figure shows an example of a hierarchical state transition diagram for a drawing tool (reference: [Dix et al., 2004]).

The following section illustrates the states for primitive interaction tasks in MDE STNs and a hierarchical STN.

3.4 PrIME Diagrammatic Notations

3.4.2 PrIME Diagrams

In this section, a hierarchical STN is presented to illustrate the primitive tasks in a multi-display environment. The more detailed STNs of different primitive tasks follow. In order to demonstrate concrete diagrams, a specific interaction technique and an input device had to be chosen. Therefore, an iPhone was selected as a potential input device for multi-display environments.

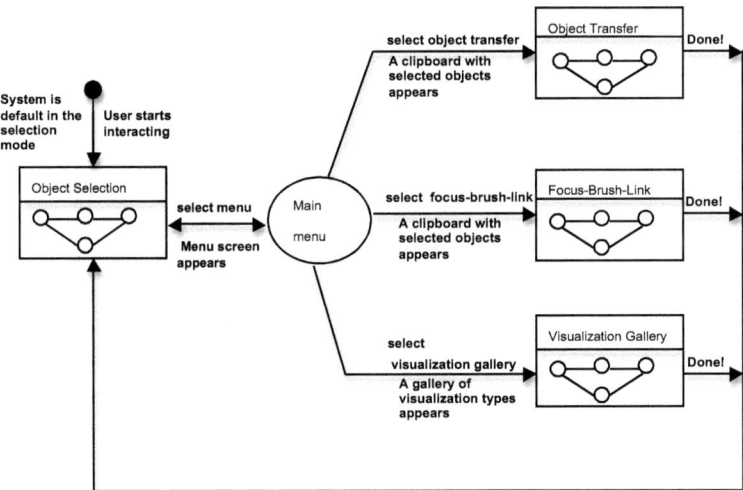

Figure 3.11: This hierarchical state transition diagram shows the a user's interaction dialogue with multiple displays to perform primitive tasks. The user's first step is to select the object of interest. After that, there are three different primitive tasks to select. The state transition networks of each primitive task are demonstrated in figures 3.12, 3.13, 3.14, 3.15 below.

The hierarchical STN in figure 3.11 below illustrates the interaction dialogue of one user with multiple displays. The first step is to select objects of interest. The detailed steps of object-selection are presented in figure 3.12 below. Afterwards, the user can choose either to transfer the objects to another display with or without keeping the link to the original object, or to generate one or more visualization diagrams for the data and present it on a target display. The hierarchical STN which is used here, helps to give a general idea about the possible primitive tasks without the complications of the detailed steps for each task.

The following diagram in figure 3.12 presents the detailed steps for selecting one or more objects from one or more displays. The steps are based on a specific interaction technique, using an iPhone as an input device. This technique is implemented and evaluated in PrIME prototype (see chapter 6).

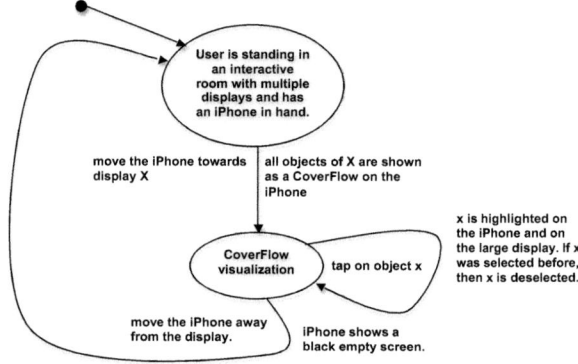

Figure 3.12: This state transition network shows the interaction dialogue of a user with multiple displays for performing object-selection tasks. The interaction technique used is based on an iPhone as an input device.

Figure 3.13 presents the object-transfer primitive task based on the interaction technique of PrIME prototype.

3.4 PrIME Diagrammatic Notations

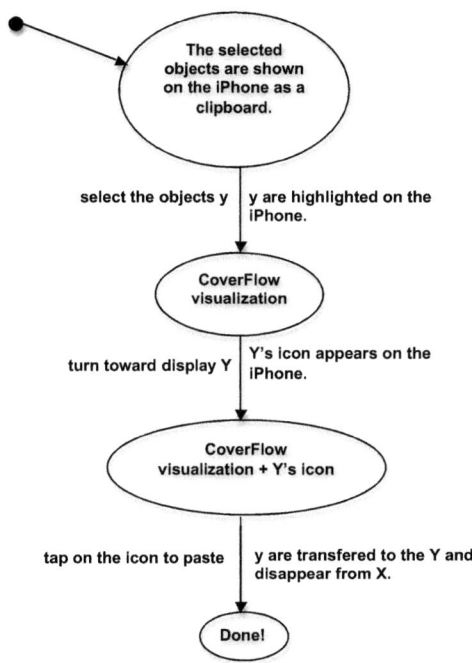

Figure 3.13: This state transition network shows the interaction dialogue of a user with multiple displays for performing object-transfer tasks. The interaction technique used is based on an iPhone as an input device. Please note that the object disappears from the original display, after being tranferred.

Figure 3.14 presents the linked object-transfer as an example of focus-brush-link primitive task.

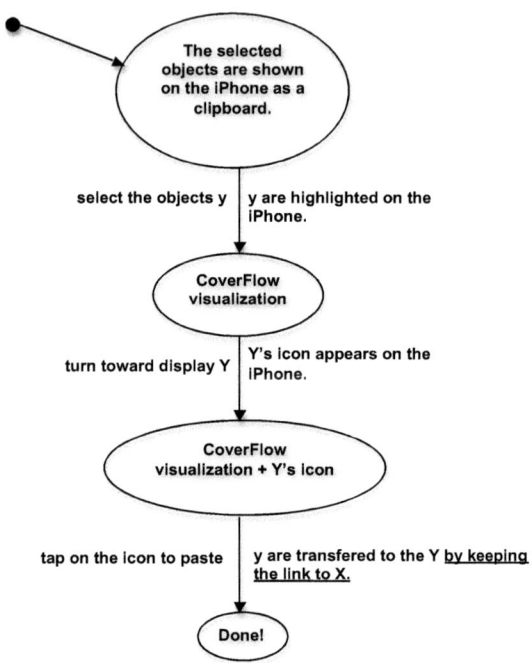

Figure 3.14: This state transition network shows the interaction dialogue of a user with multiple displays in order to perform an example of a focus-brush-link task, namely a view management task. The interaction technique used is based on an iPhone as an input device. The user can select some objects from different displays and copy them to a target display by keeping a link to the original objects on the original displays. Any changes on the target display are reflected on the original display simultaneously. Although this diagram might look identical to the previous diagram (figure 3.13), in the last step the consequence of the user's action is different. In this case, the object still remains on the original display and the new object on the target display is linked to the original one.

Figure 3.15 presents the visualization gallery as an example of an interaction task for MDEs, based on the visualization gallery primitive task in single-display environments.

3.5 Summary of the Chapter

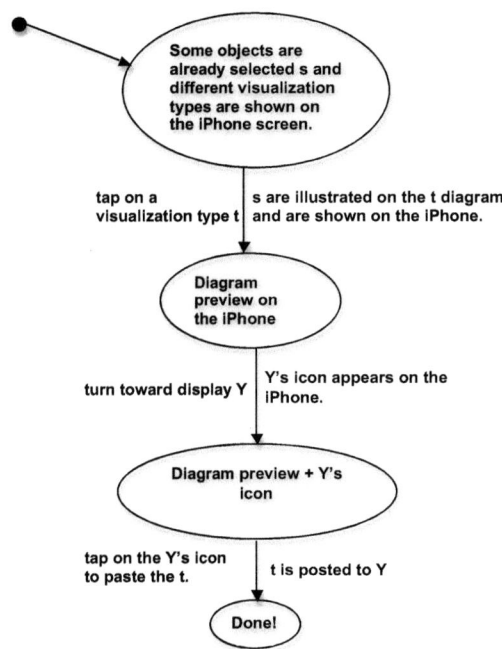

Figure 3.15: This state transition network shows a user's interaction dialogue with multiple displays for performing visualization gallery tasks. The interaction technique used is based on an iPhone as an input device.

The state transition networks presented above portray some examples of how primitive interaction tasks can be implemented in a specific scenario, using an iPhone as an input device to control multiple displays.

3.5 Summary of the Chapter

This chapter covers the theoretical parts of interaction with displays. First, a list of primitive interaction tasks in a single-display environment was mentioned, which was then extracted from current literature. This list was then extended for multi-display interaction, which can be used as an evaluation framework to compare input devices for MDEs. In addition, it guides researchers who develop novel input devices for MDEs to consider the tasks that the device should support.

Furthermore, some examples for possible interaction techniques related to each interaction task were highlighted. Finally, the last part of this chapter focused on state transition networks which use an iPhone as an input device to perform primitive interaction tasks for multi-display environments.

Chapter 4

Single-Display Interaction: CloudBrowsing Project

> *"Half of the battle in designing an interactive situated or public display is designing how the display will invite that interaction."*
>
> —Agamanolis, 2002

4.1 Introduction

The previous chapter presented state transition networks for a scenario that an iPhone is used as an input device to interact with multiple displays. Before starting with multi-user multi-display prototypes, preliminary user studies were carried out to observe how users interact with an input device with an integrated display, such as an iPhone. Researchers posed themselves the following questions: is this extra display beneficial for controlling a large display and how do users feel while using this device with regards to ergonomic issues? CloudBrowsing project gave this opportunity to answer these research questions. CloudBrowsing[1] is a scientific and artistic project in cooperation

---

[1]CloudBrowsing installation in ZKM museum Karlsruhe, German (Bernd Lintermann, Torsten Belschner, Mahsa Jenabi, Werner A. König: "CloudBrowsing" (2008-09), (c) ZKM — Karlsruhe)

with the ZKM — Center of Art and Media in Karlsruhe[2], which hold a unique position for such kind of interactive installations. In this exhibition the attempt was to shift the power to the visitors and let them control the installation. In a traditional museum visitors can enjoy masterpieces from artists and additionally read some descriptions about the works. Unfortunately, in most cases they cannot interact with the work in order to select what they are more interested in.

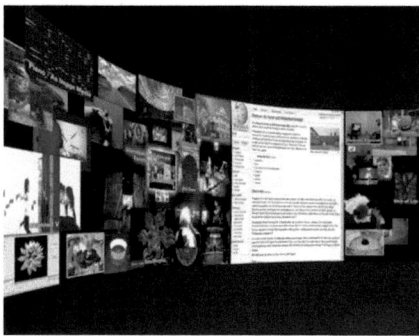

Figure 4.1: The PanoramaScreen at the ZKM — Center of Art and Media in Karlsruhe. A Wikipedia article is shown in the middle. Related images to that article are produced on the left and right sides of the Wikipedia article.

The idea of this exhibition was a new way of searching in Wikipedia by related images in addition to hypertexts. Users see a Wikipedia article in front of themselves on a panoramic display (8 meters diameter) with the related images on the left and right sides of the article (see figure 4.1 below). The application for the PanoramaScreen is implemented by colleagues at the ZKM Museum. The role of the researchers of the HCI group at the University of Konstanz was to design and implement the user interaction for controlling the panoramic display. The next section specifies the requirements for this installation.

---
[2]www.zkm.de

4.2 Requirement Engineering

Given was a large panoramic display with a pre-implemented application. The challenge was to choose a proper input device that could control the application. Furthermore, it should support visitors at the museum that have different background knowledge and are of different ages to understand without any supplementary clarifications. The application is for single users, meaning only one person (active user) at a time can use the input device; but, it is also important to entertain the observers (passive users) who are not holding the input device, yet can communicate with the active user and suggest specific tasks. The interaction must be mobile, since the large panoramic display requires freedom of movement for the users.

An iPhone was chosen, since it facilitates the simple touch interaction and mobility. Additionally, it has an integrated display, own processor, and a rich set of sensors such as a vibration sensor, microphone, accelerometer, which give researchers many possibilities to design an intuitive interaction. Other mobile devices such as TabletPCs also have many of these features, but they are heavier to carry. The following section illustrates the technical set-up of the CloudBrowsing in a lab environment, as well as in a museum.

4.3 Technical Set-up

The input device is a black case that includes an iPod Touch or iPhone (see figure 4.2 below). An orientation sensor, called inertia cube sensor[3] is also included next to the iPod Touch. This sensor can specify the orientation of the device (user) in 360 degrees. It is also used for moving the pointer on the screen. This bodily interaction attempts to simulate the familiar interaction of people to the physical world. An iPod Touch was used for the installation just because it is cheaper than an iPhone. Furthermore, the installation room in ZKM was not ready in the beginning; therefore, the Media Room at the University of Konstanz (see figure 4.3 below) was used for the purpose of

---

[3]InterSense Inc. InterSense InertiaCube2: http://www.intersense.com/InertiaCube_Sensors.asp

development and evaluation. More details about the technical set-up in the Media Room is explained in the following section.

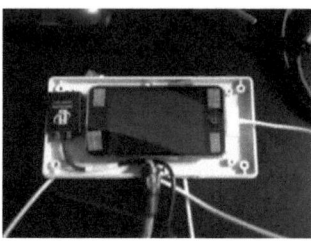

Figure 4.2: The input device is a black case that includes an iPod Touch or iPhone and an orientation sensor called inertia cube sensor.

4.3.1 Media Room

The input device used was identical to the one in the real museum. Yet instead of a 360° panoramic display two large Eyevis Cube display were used with rear-projection, 67-inch, and 1980 * 1200 pixel resolution (see figure 4.4 and 4.5 below). These two large displays represented one part of the panoramic display. The development of the prototype and the first and second user studies were carried out in this environment. The technical set-up in the museum is illustrated in the next section.

4.3.2 PanoramaLab at the ZKM

The installation included a 360° PanoramaScreen at the ZKM[4]. It has 8 meters diameter and is 2.80 meters high. Six projectors are configured for this display and the resolution is 1400 * 1050 pixels. The input device, which is compacted inside the black case, is initially located on a stand in the middle of the room (see figure 4.6 below). The iPhone plays a guide video about the way one should use the iPhone. The videos show only the iPhone screen and the hand of a user, who is interacting with it, selecting different buttons, and using different features. This

---
[4]http://on1.zkm.de/zkm/stories/storyReader$5803

4.3 Technical Set-up

Figure 4.3: This figure shows the Media Room at the University of Konstanz. This experimental lab is a great place for prototyping and testing novel interaction techniques.

Figure 4.4: This figure shows the two Eyevis Cube displays that are used instead of the panoramic display for developing and evaluating issues.

Figure 4.5: This figure illustrates the Media Room setting which was used for primary evaluation of the CloudBrowsing prototype.

helps the users to learn about the possible controls of the device. As the user takes the input device in his or her hand, the mode changes to the navigation mode, which means the user can point and select on the PanoramaScreen.

The next section presents the interaction design process and highlights its challenges and the solutions that were discovered.

Figure 4.6: This figure illustrates the input device in the ZKM Museum. The device was placed on a stand in the middle of the room. The iPod Touch played a guide video to help the users understand the interaction method. As users take the device in their hand, the mode changes to navigation mode, wherein the user can point and select.

4.4 Design Process

New design challenges for multiple displays

Having two displays in our installation (PanoramaScreen and the iPhone screen) opened up a new challenge of how to distribute information between these displays efficiently. Mobile phones have already been used as input devices by other researchers. Chan et al. [2005] have used an orientation-aware handheld device in a museum that assist visitors in locating an exhibit easier. In [Eissele et al., 2004], a prototype is implemented with a TabletPC in addition to an InertiaCube sensor that displays a virtual object at the same location and orientation as the real-world object. The user can explore the object from different views by moving the display around the object without any need to move the object itself (see chapter 2 for more related projects).

4.4 Design Process

Figure 4.7: CloudBrowsing installation in ZKM museum (Bernd Lintermann, Torsten Belschner, Mahsa Jenabi, Werner A. König: "CloudBrowsing" (2008-09), (c) ZKM — Karlsruhe).

In the CloudBrowsing project, the problem of multiple displays was solved through the application of an iterative design process. Three iterations are taken to realize the final prototype. In each iteration the implemented prototype is evaluated by a user study or a focus group. The results of the study are interpreted and decisions are made for improvements. In the next part, the first iteration of the design process is explained.

4.4.1 Prototype 1

This section highlights the design of the interaction with the iPhone. Furthermore, it presents the results of the expert focus group that tested the application. The feedback from the focus group led to improvements, which are explained in the prototype 2 section.

Design

Image Selection
When users point to an image of interest, they can see a small icon of that image on the iPhone screen (see figures 4.8 and 4.9 below). Selecting the image is done by a tap of a finger, which consequently opens the corresponding Wikipedia article and generates the related images to that article dynamically.

While clicking on an image, the pointer on the image shortly changes its shape and the selected image is presented enlarged and highlighted with a red frame around it (see figure 4.8 below). This gives users a visual feedback for their actions.

Figure 4.8: When users point to an image of interest, they can see a small icon of that image on the iPhone screen. To select the image, users only need to tap on the icon. Consequently, the related Wikipedia article opens on the PanoramaScreen and the selected image remains highlighted, with a red frame and enlargement, as a visual feedback for the users.

Search
A search function enables users to input keywords and search directly in Wikipedia by using the iPhone virtual keyboard (see figure 4.10 below). As they type in a keyword, the article corresponding to the first result is shown on the PanoramaScreen. Moreover, other results are listed on the iPhone that can be selected on demand (see figure 4.11 below). Entering keywords on a personal iPhone display is also more convenient for users: they can take more time to correct words or simply to remember a keyword, and they do not feel that they are being watched.

Related Images
Other features include: if a pointer stays on an image (dwell),

4.4 Design Process

Figure 4.9: This figure shows the User Interface (UI) of the iPhone in the pointing mode. The image which is currently under the pointer is shown, as well as the title of the related Wikipedia article and a part of the description of the image. The two buttons on the top right-hand side are the search button and the history button.

 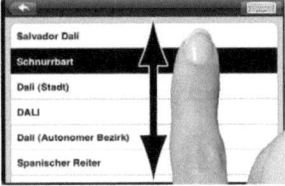

Figure 4.10: This figure shows a snapshot of the iPhone screen designed for searching keywords.

Figure 4.11: After users enter a keyword, the results are listed on the iPhone as pictured above.

associated images are presented on the iPhone display. In one glance, nine thumbnails of the images can be seen (see figure 4.12 below). Therefore, the user can select other images or continue navigating by moving the device. These related images do exist on the PanoramaScreen as well, but it takes more time to find them for the user because of the information overload (abundance of images).

Scrolling
When users point to the Wikipedia page, the Wikipedia article is also shown on the iPhone (see figure 4.13 below). Moving the finger from the bottom to the top, scrolls the page up on the PanoramaScreen, as well as on the iPhone and vice versa. Swiping to the left side presents the previous article and to the

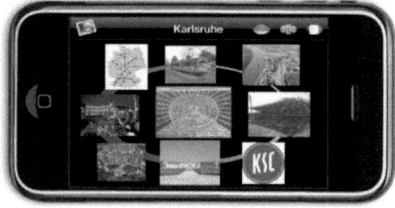

Figure 4.12: Through keeping the pointer situated on an image (dwelling), relevant images are presented on the iPhone display. In one glance, nine thumbnails of the images can be seen.

right the next article.

Hyperlinks
At first, it was not clear how to show the Wikipedia hyperlinks on the iPhone. One alternative was to divide the UI into two parts. One part would scroll the Wikipedia page up and down, and the other would list the hyperlinks (see figure 4.14 below). The list of links is generated from the links that the user has recently run over with the mouse. Since the users' focus is always switching between the PanoramaScreen and the iPhone, it is hard to look at the iPhone and select a link from the list of links without moving the iPhone, and accidentally changing the mode. The solution was that after the user dwells on a link, just this links is shown as a text overlay on the Wikipedia page. Tapping on the link opens the related Wikipedia article on the PanoramaScreen (see figure 4.15 below).

History
To give the users a clue on what topics the previous visitors were interested in, there is a menu item called history. Through selecting this item, the user can see all the images that were

4.4 Design Process

Figure 4.13: When users point to the Wikipedia page, the Wikipedia article is also shown on the iPhone. Moving the finger on an upwards direction, scrolls the page on the PanoramaScreen down, as well as on the iPhone and vice versa. Swiping to the left side presents the previous article and to the right the next article. The hyperlinks that the user hovered with the mouse are shown as a list over the Wikipedia page. In the final design just one hyperlink is shown as soon as the user points to a hyperlink on the PanoramaScreen (see figure 4.15 below).

selected before and has a chance to select them again.

Help
There were three types of aids for the users to learn how the installation can be managed. The first one is the guide video played on the iPhone, while it is in its initial position on the stand. Secondly, a display outside the room shows a video of a user while he or she is interacting with the system (see figure 4.16 below). Finally, a poster is hanging outside the room that lists all the functions with a brief explanation of each one (see Appendix B).

Three types of help for the visitors

4 Single-Display Interaction: CloudBrowsing Project

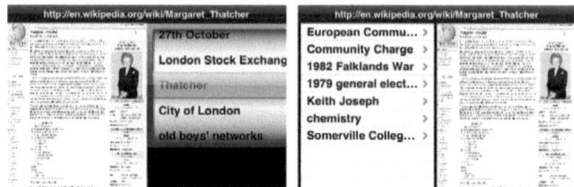

Figure 4.14: Two design prototypes for presenting the hyperlinks that the user has hovered with the pointer on the iPhone screen. The final decision of the presentation of this GUI is shown in figure 4.15 below

Figure 4.15: The final version of how to show the hyperlinks on the iPhone.

Implementation

The application of the iPhone is implemented in Objective C. The iPhone is connected to the panorama server via Wireless LAN and sends the interaction events to the server and the server responds to these events by changing the GUI of the PanoramaScreen (see figure 4.17 below). The messages are sent via UDP in XML format. Images are sent to the iPhone via TCP. The application for the InertiaCube sensor, as well a the animation on the PanoramaScreen, are implemented by ZKM (see the credits in appendix A). When users select an image, the panorama server presents the related Wikipedia article on the PanoramaScreen. Additionally, the title of the article is searched in yahoo, restricted to Wikimedia [5] to find the images related to the selected image. The related images are generated dynamically and presented on the left- and right-hand sides of the Wikipedia article.

---

[5] http://www.wikimedia.de

4.4 Design Process

Figure 4.16: This figure show the area outside the installation room. A display was mounted at the entrance, which represented a video of a user while she was interacting with the system.

The next section presents the evaluation of the first prototype.

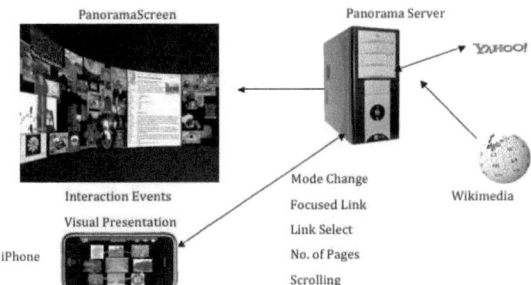

Figure 4.17: This figure illustrates the architecture of the CloudBrowsing.

Evaluation

To evaluate the first prototype, a focus group was formed. Three experts from the Human-Computer Interaction group of the University of Konstanz came together to test the system and review the usability issues. Since the installation room in the museum was not ready yet, the review took place in the Media Room at the University. The experts were introduced to the

Problems by dwelling

interaction technique and had a chance to test the device and all of its functionalities. Afterwards, a discussion took place about the technique's advantages and disadvantages. The experts came to the conclusion that showing related images by dwelling on the image for some seconds is not efficient, since this function cannot easily be found by the users. In addition, any accidental dwelling on an image would trigger the related images on the small screen. This decreases the responsiveness of the system, because all the related images are sent to the iPhone each time the pointer dwells on an image. Thus, the prototype was improved in a way that the related images are only shown, if the image is already selected by the user (again by dwelling on the selected image).

Small icons

Another problem was that the icons of the related images on the iPhone were considered to be too small. Yet, small images without any text information cannot help users to navigate and find their topic of interest. The solution to this problem is to present the images as a CoverFlow visualization (see figure 4.18 below). The advantage is that the images can be enlarged along with their titles.

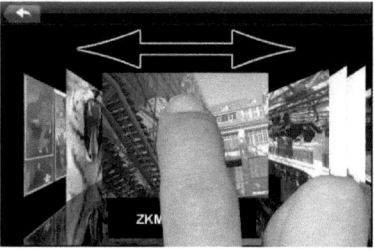

Figure 4.18: A CoverFlow visualization of the related images on the iPhone. This representation of the images has the advantage that the images are bigger and more recognizable for users. Furthermore, the title of the image is also show on the bottom part of the GUI.

There was another problem that needed to be fixed. Switching the focus between the two displays may increase the cognitive load and confuse the users. Therefore researchers tried to implement blind interaction wherever possible in the interaction method. That means although the images on the iPhone screen do not take the whole iPhone screen (there might be some black spaces around the image), wherever the user taps with

4.4 Design Process

his finger, this image will be selected. In this case the user can just continue watching the PanoramaScreen and tap blindly on the iPhone. The same solution was applied to the selection of the hyperlinks. Wherever the user taps on the iPhone, this link will be selected. Blind interaction is not desirable for all of the UI modes, since sometimes the user needs to see the extra information, for example in order to see related images or to enter keywords to search.

Blind interaction

4.4.2 Prototype 2

According to the results of the focus group, the prototype was improved in the second iteration of the design process. The changes are mentioned in the following section. The new prototype was evaluated by a user study in the Media Room. This evaluation design is explained in the evaluation section.

Design

By selecting an image on the iPhone, the relevant images are represented in a CoverFlow presentation on the iPhone. Therefore, the user can select other images or continue navigating by moving the device. Blind interaction is realized in some situations such as for selecting an image of interest or for selecting a hyperlink. In these cases the user can blindly touch the iPhone's screen, while continually looking at the PanoramaScreen.

Blind interaction for selecting images and hyperlinks

In order to prevent users from missing the information presented on the iPhone, a short vibration feedback can be felt. The iPhone vibrates each time to notify the user that there is additional information on the iPhone to view.

As the improvements were implemented, a user study was carried out to test the usability of the interaction with users. The next section explains the design of the experiment.

Evaluation

A user study was carried out to check, if the interaction concept and GUI are understandable and usable for the users. Thirteen users (7 female/6 male, 12-41 years old) participated. Six of them acted as single users and three groups were created (including two groups of two and one group of three people). Groups of people were also tested, since in the real museum exhibition, both cases of single or a group of users can visit the installation. None of the users owned an iPhone or an iPod Touch, six of them had never tried it before. The others did not have much experience with an iPhone. With the real setting of the museum with the PanoramaScreen not ready, the museum setting was simulated in the Media Room with two Eyevis Cubes displays instead of the PanoramaScreen, as mentioned before, using the identical input device as that of the museum (illustrated in figure 4.4). Firstly users had the chance to play around with the device and figure out its functionality without any explanation. Then, they filled out a qualitative questionnaire about their background knowledge, as well as their impression of the system and interaction, with the new form of input device. Afterwards, the moderator explained the users the functionalities of the device and let them try again. Finally, the users filled in another questionnaire about their impression of the interaction technique after the moderator's explanation.

Usability test in the Media Room

Five single users had a chance to test the system with and without a vibration feedback. The input device vibrated each time that the iPhone was presenting the related images.

The results of the evaluation are pictured in the following section.

Result

77%(10/13) of the users could understand the image navigation via input device relative quickly. One person did not understood the idea and had to have it explained to him. 77% (10/13) of the users figured out the search functionality, but just 23% (3/13) noticed the function of visualizing related images on the iPhone (see diagram 4.19 below). Concerning exhaustion of fingers, hands or arms. 69% (9/13) had no inconvenience with

4.4 Design Process

the device. 31% (4/13) had a slightly tired hand. One person felt that his arms were semi tired. All of the users mentioned that the interaction was fun and easy, as soon as they knew which functions exist. 85% (11/13) mentioned that the functionality of summarizing related images on the iPhone is important and helpful for further navigation. 77% (10/13) said that the search function was easy to use. 92% (12/13) would use iPhone again as an input device. The average of system accuracy was mentioned as 52%, before clarifying the interaction method, after which it increased to 65%. A similar effect had clarification about the speed of the input device. People mentioned the speed of the input device as 74% high, which increased after clarification to 84%. This shows that clarifying how a system works would give the users a better feeling of having the system under control and also finding the system more accurate and with higher responsiveness. The average grade for the application from the scale of 1 to 6 (1 being the best grade) was 1.76.

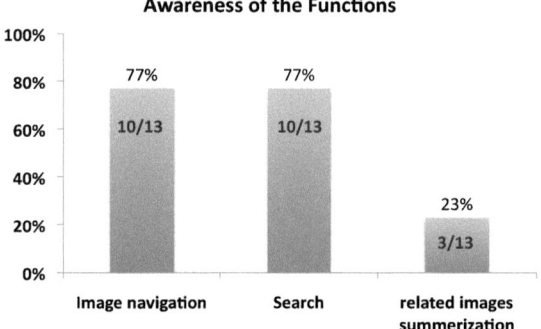

Figure 4.19: This diagram shows how many percent of the users were aware of each of the three functionalities: navigating by images, searching keywords, related images as a summary on the iPhone (this was before they received clarification from the moderator). Visualization of the related images on the iPhone was only noticed by three people out of thirteen. Therefore, in the next iteration of the design process this problem was solved by showing a dummy screenshot of the iPhone on the PanoramaScreen (see figure 4.22 below)

Users did not understand the meaning of vibration feedback and thought something was wrong. They found vibration to be an

Vibration effect

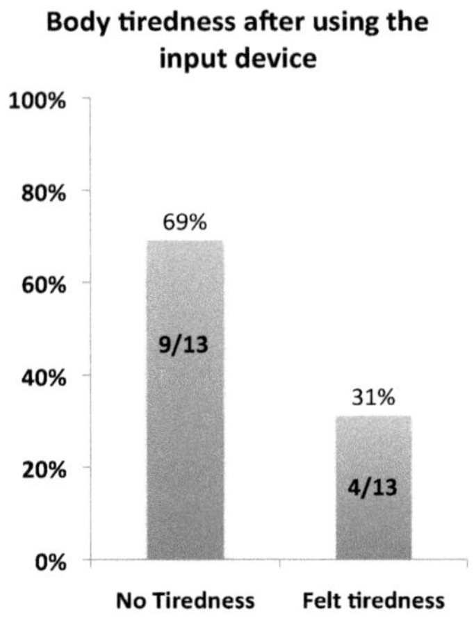

Body tiredness after using the input device

- No Tiredness: 69% (9/13)
- Felt tiredness: 31% (4/13)

Figure 4.20: This figure illustrates the opinion of the thirteen users about the tiredness caused by using the input device. Nine users mentioned that the input device was not tiring at all. Four other users had a light tiredness in hand and arm.

aggressive kind of feedback. Therefore it was eliminated for the museum exhibition.

The swiping interaction for scrolling was ignored by the users. Since most people did not own an iPhone, they could not find the way that they can scroll, so this type of interaction was replaced by visible arrow keys to scroll up and down (see figure 4.21 below). This cleared up the difference of designing iPhone use for a museum exhibition and an everyday application because for an everyday-use application, the designer can suppose that users know all the standard Apple iPhone's touch interactions. Yet museum visitors may not own such a device and might not know the predefined touch interactions. They need to figure this out for themselves in a short time. Visible controls can help in these cases. The same decision was made for back and forward functions in the Wikipedia browser. Two arrow keys replaced the predefined iPhone interaction of dragging the finger to the left or right on the screen. The two arrow keys on the left and right-hand sides show the previous or next Wikipedia article, as is standard

Invisible controls for scrolling

4.4 Design Process

in most of Internet browsers such as Firefox browser.

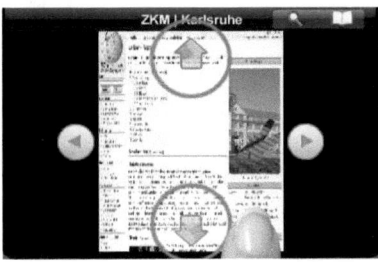

Figure 4.21: Visible controls were added to the GUI to make it visible for the users. Up and down arrow keys scroll the Wikipedia article on the iPhone, as well as on the PanoramaScreen up and down. The left and right arrow keys go back and forward as standard in most of Internet browsers, such as Firefox.

4.4.3 Prototype 3

According to the lessons learned from the user study, the prototype was improved in the third iteration of the design process. The challenges of the next iteration are explained below.

Design

In this prototype the vibration feature was eliminated because of the negative feedback from the users. Visible controls (arrow keys) were implemented for scrolling and going back and forward in the Wikipedia article. In order to help the users recognize when they should switch their focus to the iPhone display, a dummy screenshot of the iPhone was shown on the PanoramaScreen. This dummy user interface shows the current mode of the iPhone UI. For example, if the user clicks on an image, a screen shot of the input device is shown on PanoramaScreen with the CoverFlow visualization of some dummy images. Therefore, the user knows that the related images are shown on the iPhone (see figure 4.22 below).

Dummy screenshot of the iPhone on the PanoramaScreen

4 Single-Display Interaction: CloudBrowsing Project

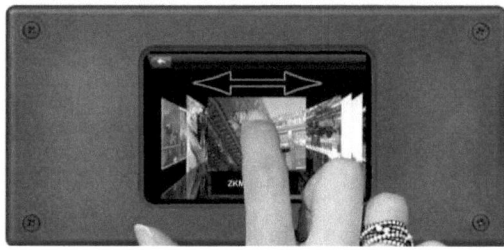

Figure 4.22: A dummy screenshot of the iPhone (highlighted above with a green circle) is shown on the PanoramaScreen in order to notify the user that some extra information is shown on the iPhone.

Preliminary Evaluation in the Museum

A few days before the opening of the real exhibition room in the museum a user study was carried out to check if the improvements of the third iteration have solved the noticed problems. Three single users participated and the result showed that they noticed all of the functionalities without any clarifications.

In addition to the user study, some questionnaires were left at the museum for the volunteer visitors to fill out in order for them to report about their experience of the installation. Seven people (all male, 23-67 years old) filled it out. Just one of them owned an iPhone and used it very often; the rest had never had or tried it before. Four out of seven understood the interaction concept immediately, 29% (2/7) in average time and 14% (1/7) relatively

4.4 Design Process

late. 86% (6/7) determined the input device as very accurate and one person average in accuracy. Our average grade for the installation was 1.33. Only 29%(2/7) of the users had read the guide poster at the entrance.

Interdisciplinary User study in the Museum

In cooperation with Mrs. Dr. Katrin Allmendinger, who is a guest researcher from the field of Psychology, a user study was carried out in the museum. This study was carried out to, on the one hand, answer the research question: which way of navigation (related images, hyperlinks, or keywords for searching) is preferable for the users to search about a topic? On the other hand, it was carried out to discover, in the content of social science, how does cooperation work between two users that are searching for a topic together. Furthermore, the study was to look at which person is more dominant and more influential: the active user, who has the input device in hand, or the passive user, who has no input device, but can communicate with the active user and influence his or her actions. Concerning interaction design, people were also asked about the usability of the input device.

Participants of the user study were visitors of the museum. Ten single users, ten Dyads (15-67 years old, $M = 31.37$, of which half were men) were tested. For the case of dyads, one person was randomly chosen to use the input device (active user). It was not allowed for the passive user to use the input device during the experiment. In the beginning the users filled out a questionnaire about their background knowledge of iPhone/iPod or touch displays as well as their experiences with panoramic displays. After, the moderator clarified how the system works by searching for information about the city "New York". Then, users had ten minutes time to find information about Tehran, the capital city of Iran. As they were finished with the task, they filled out two further questionnaires. The first one was about their impression of the system and the input device and the second questionnaire included some questions about Tehran. The aim of the second questionnaire was to measure the learning effect for single users and dyads as a between factor and also in dyads, for active users versus passive users as a within factor.

Navigation	Related Images	Hyperlinks	Keywords
Mean	7.1	12.4	0.7
SD	7.1	3.8	1.0

Table 4.1: The table lists the means and standard deviations of navigation possibilities.

The active user had three possibilities to get more information about the topic, namely by entering search keywords, selecting related images, and/or selecting the hyperlinks inside the Wikipedia article as a text or an image. The number of related-images selections, searching by keywords, or clicking on hyperlink texts or images inside the Wikipedia were stored as a log file. The mean values and standard deviations are shown in the table 4.1 below.

Questionnaire data shows that users had fun with the installation (Scale 1 (Not at all) - 7 (very much): M = 6.4, SD = 0.7)
Users tendency to navigate through images was (Scale 1 (Not at all) - 7 (very much)): M=5.97, SD= 1.066, and for navigation via text: M= 4.63, SD= 1.402.
A Paired-Sampling T-test shows that users tend significantly more to navigate via images: t(29) = 4.085, p= 0.000, $\alpha = 0.05$. The result of the Tehran questionnaire shows that from the maximum points of 7, people success was M = 3.9, SD = 1.2 (ANOVA was not significant: f(2,26) = 0.391, P = 0.680). Users were asked how proper was the installation for informal learning (Scale 1 (Not at all) - 7 (very much)): M = 6.0, SD = 1.2). The ANOVA test was significant (F(2, 27)= 3.635 P = 0.04); especially the passive users of the Dyad said that it is very proper (M = 6.7, SD= 0.483). Users liked the installation very much (Scale 1 (Not at all) - 7 (very much)): M = 6.4, SD = 0.9) and liked the input device (Scale 1 (Not at all) - 7 (very much)): M = 5.8, SD = 1.2: only active and single users were asked)

Here are some questions posed to the single users about their interaction with the input device for the single users:

- How was the usage of the input device? M = 5.70, SD = 1.494 (Scale 1 (very hard) - 7 (very easy))

- How easy was it for you to understand how the input

4.4 Design Process

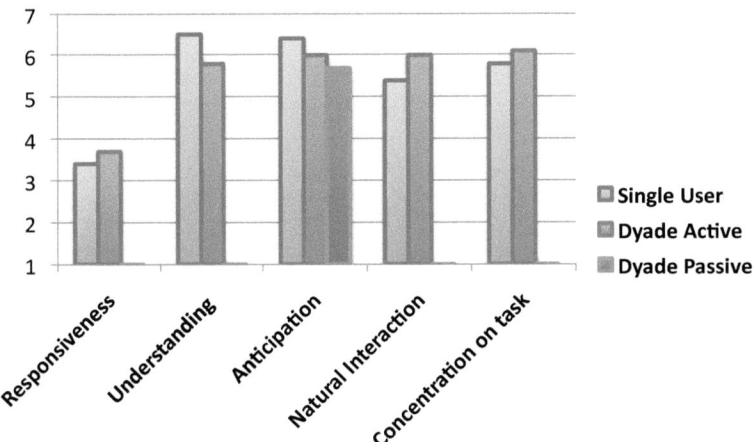

Figure 4.23: This diagram illustrates the result of the questionnaire data. Users answered the questions by a scale of 1 (very low) - 7 (very high).

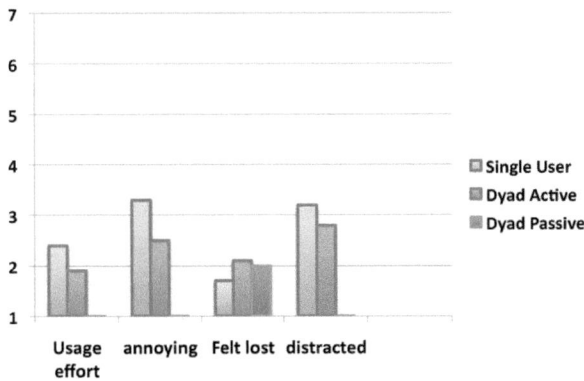

Figure 4.24: This diagram illustrates the result of the questionnaire data. Users answered the questions by a scale of 1 (very low) - 7 (very high).

device works? M = 6.50, SD = 0.850 (Scale 1 (very hard) - 7 (very easy))

- How quick was the reaction of the system after your input? M = 3.40, SD = 0.699 (Scale 1 (too slow) - 4 (exactly correct) - 7 (too quick))

- Did you navigate more via images or text? M = 3.10, SD = 1.449 (Scale 1 (via image) - 4 (both) - 7 (via text))

Some questions were asked to the dyads about the cooperation between the users:

- Up to what extent did you feel that you are influencing the task of searching for Tehran in Wikipedia? (Scale 1 (Not at all) - 7 (very high): active users : M = 5.2, SD = 1.8; passive users: M = 6.1, SD = 0.9)

- Which one of you had the feeling that he or she is more dominant in the teamwork? (Scale 1 (Me) - 7 (My partner): active users : M = 4.1, SD = 2.1; passive users: M = 4.5, SD = 1.6)

- Would an additional input device be helpful, so that you could control the system at the same time? (Scale 1 (Not at all)- 4(moderately helpful) - 7 (very helpful): active users : M = 4.1, SD = 2.1; passive users: M = 4.1, SD = 2.6)

- Did you navigate more via images or text? Passive users: M = 3.50, SD = 1.581 (Scale 1 (via image) - 4 (both) - 7 (via text)) Active users: M = 3.30, SD = 1.567.

4.5 Lessons Learned

In all people had fun with the application. They liked the input device and learned the way of interacting and searching for a topic quickly. Navigation via images and hyperlinks was used more than searching through keywords. Active and passive users could accomplish the task cooperatively without any problems. They did not find it necessary to have two input devices, so that each person can interact directly with the system.

4.5 Lessons Learned

Using input devices with their own display, such as Apple iPhone, opens new challenges to the HCI field. It is an important design decision to choose what information should be presented on which display and how the user can become aware of which display he should look at. On the one hand having more than one display can help the users' interaction by distributing the information physically among displays (cognitive partitioning); on the other hand, an uneducated design can even increase the cognitive load and confuse the user. The dominancy of the display plays an important role in designing its UI. In CloudBrowsing, the PanoramaScreen is much more dominant because of its size in comparison with the iPhone screen and consequently the users look more at it and sometimes oversee the information presented on the iPhone. The user study showed that before clarifying the interaction method users miss some information presented on the iPhone, since they focus more on the PanoramaScreen. But as the moderator explained how the interaction technique works, they learn it quickly are able to use it without any problems. This shows that distributed focus on multiple display is acceptable and efficient when users know when to look at which display and is not surprised by the system. This lesson was applied to the next prototype (explained in chapter 6), where the primitive tasks are done via an iPhone. There, any primitive action is started from the user and therefore users know when they should look at which display.

Challenges of using an input device with an integrated display

Although using an orientation sensor brought the application closer to the familiar interaction of users with their environment, it made it also more sensitive to the movements of the user. Hence, small body movements by the user would have a direct influence on the UI, which made it hard for the user to show something to the person accompanying him or her. One solution could be to have a way of fixating the UI on demand, for example, a specific button on the device, which freezes the display. Another solution might be, putting the finger on the touch display and keep it there during the time the user wants to fixate the UI. Barkhuus and Dey [2003] have studied whether the context-aware applications take control away from the users. They concluded: "users are willing to accept a large degree of autonomy from applications, as long as the application's usefulness is greater than the cost of limited control." To avoid this problem in the next prototype (explained in chapter 6) the object selection on the iPhone is designed in a way that the iPhone screen shows all the objects on a display and not just one object,

Body interaction and user's uncertainty

at which the cursor is pointing.

Mobile keyboard

In addition, researchers found that the iPhone's virtual keyboard is useful as a mobile keyboard that can support text input. Ergonomically carrying an iPhone as an input device was acceptable for the test subjects, to the point that they could imagine using it for controlling their environment in everyday applications. The small screen of iPhone limits interaction designers in showing many objects, however the decision of using the CoverFlow visualization gave the opportunity to show icons of related images in an acceptable size with extra information (i.e., title of the related Wikipedia article).

Users' acceptance of the interface justified that the iPhone is a potential input device that can be used also for the next prototype, which controls multiple displays.

4.6 Summary of the Chapter

This chapter reported about the experiences of designing, implementing, and evaluating a prototype in the ZKM museum. An iPhone in addition to an orientation sensor (InertiaCube sensor) were used as an input device to control a 360° panoramic display (PanoramaScreen at ZKM). The design challenges of the interaction concept are highlighted, as well as the solutions. The result showed that users enjoyed the interaction while using the new input device. The lessons learned from the user studies helped to extend the interaction to multiple displays, more than one active users in the next prototype (chapter 6).

Chapter 5

Methodology

> *"People Propose, Science Studies, Technology Conforms."*
>
> —Donald Norman in Things That Make Us Smart

Does a mobile input device with an integrated display improve performing cross-display interaction tasks? This chapter discusses the practical approach used to answer this research question.

For this research work a working prototype is built and evaluated which includes two types of interaction, namely object selection and object transfer. The devices used were an iPhone, as a representative mobile device with an integrated display, as well as a laser-pointing device without a display. Additionally, by attaching markers to the iPhone and to the laser-pointing device (see figure 5.1 belows), the system used was aware of the orientation and position of the user (device), through the OptiTrack tracking system[1]. This information was used to control the cursor and to recognize on which display the user was focusing.

This research was carried out in the experimental lab of the Human Computer Interaction group at the University of Konstanz, which is called Media Room. Section 5.1 in this chapter discusses the technical set up used whereas section 5.2

---

[1] http://www.naturalpoint.com/optitrack/

discusses and compares the variety of input devices used for MDEs. Furthermore, the functionality of the Optitrack system is demonstrated in section 5.3 and finally section 5.4 highlights the technical set-up used for the selected input devices, namely the iPhone and the laser-pointing device.

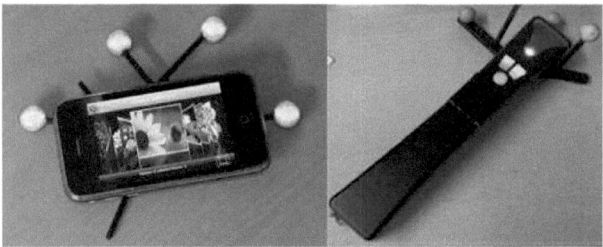

Figure 5.1: The iPhone and the laser-pointing device with markers.

5.1 Media Room Setting

The Media Room is located at the Human-Computer Interaction Group of the University of Konstanz (see figure 5.2). It is an experimental lab for designing, implementing, and evaluating novel interaction techniques. An Optitrack tracking system (a vision-based tracking system) is installed, including 12 cameras. Different vertical and horizontal large displays enable multi-user collaborative settings. Three displays of the Media Room were used for this research, namely: an Eyevis Cube display with rear-projection, 67-inch, and 1980 * 1200 pixels resolution, a Microsoft Surface touch table, 30-inch, and 1024*768 pixels resolution as well as an NEC HD display with 40-inch, and 1980*1200 pixels resolution. The Media Room is also equipped with different kinds of input devices. For the purpose of this research, the researchers made use of an iPhone 4 and a laser-pointing device, the reason for which will be discussed further in the following section, 5.2.

5.2 Input Devices for MDEs

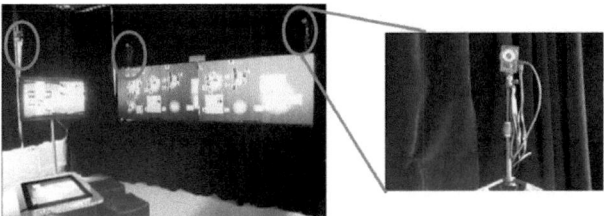

Figure 5.2: The Media Room of the HCI group at the University of Konstanz. 12 Optitrack cameras are installed all over the room.

5.2 Input Devices for MDEs

When it comes to interacting with co-located multiple displays, the challenge is to decide which input device would fit best. Table 5.1 below lists a variety of input devices, along with their advantages and disadvantages. For instance, one drawback of using a digital pen, laser pointer, mouse & keyboard as well as hand-free gestures in comparison to a mobile phone is that the user has no privacy, since the feedback of the system is public. Privacy is an important issue, especially when entering passwords. According to studies by [Brignull and Rogers, 2003] social embarrassment is a barrier for people interacting with large public displays. People fear making mistakes which are shown on the display and which will make them look foolish in the eyes of the on-looking audience [Finke et al., 2008]. One example is when people want to enter a search-keyword (see chapter 4). On the other hand, a laser pointer, a mobile phone, and hand-free gestures can all be used for remote interaction. The user is free for movements while interacting with the system. However, hand-free gestures are demanding, since people have to memorize the interaction gestures. In comparison, a mobile phone and a laser pointer can offer visible controls. However, the interaction design for these devices is challenging. A bad design for a mobile phone or a laser pointer can also increase the chance of confusing the user when the commands to the system require the user to carry out complex in-the-air movements (gestures) with the device.

Comparing potential Input Devices for MDEs

In order to answer the research question mentioned earlier in section 1.1 of this thesis, the researcher decided to compare two devices, one of which had an integrated display whereas the other did not have one. The Apple iPhone 4 was selected as a representative device with an integrated display, since it has a relatively big touch screen (3.5-inch diagonal widescreen with 960*640-pixel resolution at 326 ppi). The simple touch interaction enhances the user experience. Additional sensors integrated in the iPhone, such as a gyroscope, camera, accelerometer, microphone and light sensor, increase its potential to improve the interaction technique. For instance, it can adapt to the users' requirements. When the user puts this device on a touch table, it can react as a token[2]. As soon as the user increases his or her distance from a display, the iPhone can be used as a remote controller. This is especially helpful for handicapped users. Using a mobile phone as a personal device is common for the user and this device holds the user's information and preferences. Such information can be used to adapt the system to the user's interests. Furthermore, the user can save the data on his mobile phone and take it home. Other high quality mobile devices such as iPad and tablet PCs can also be used. However, the iPhone is lighter and can be easily used for other purposes, such as as a remote controller.

A laser-pointing device was selected as a representative device without a display. The reason was that a laser-pointing device enables mobile and remote interaction, which makes it comparable to the iPhone. The laser pointer used was developed by Werner König, Human-Computer Interaction group at the University of Konstanz [König et al., 2008]. The original laser pointer sends infrared light to infrared cameras and so it can control the mouse for a single display. In this research another method is used to track the laser pointer, namely by attaching markers and using the Optitrack system. The reason behind this was to use the same technique as with the iPhone, so as to make the comparison between the devices valid. More details about the tracking technique is presented in the following section.

---

[2]Physical object, which has been augmented by Microsoft's Surface byte tags

5.3 Display Recognition

12 Optitrack cameras are installed in the Media Room (see figure 5.2 above). This vision-based tracking system can track passive and active infrared reflective markers (refer to figure 5.1 above). Position, orientation, and target-ID information is produced as the output, which can be used to recognize the direction in which the user (the device) is facing. In this way, the projection of a line, defined by the orientation and position of the device on a display is calculated. The point of intersection is defined as the mouse/cursor pointer on the screen. While the user moves the device to the left or right, up or down, the cursor pointer moves respectively. If the user faces a display-free space between the displays, the visual feedback of the cursor on the screen disappears. A solution for bridging this gap is presented in section 6.4.

5.4 Technical Infrastructure

The iPhone and the laser-pointing device are tracked by the Optitrack cameras, as explained in the previous section. The markers were attached to the input device so that the orientation of the device could be recognized by the Optitrack system. The squidy framework is used (more details in [Rädle, 2010], [König, 2010], [König et al., 2010]) to connect the Optitrack to the server and map the commands to specific actions of the system.

Squidy is an interaction library [3] for multi-modal input devices (see fig. 5.3 below). The GUI of Squidy enables programmers to add different modalities to the pipeline of the program. One advantage of Squidy is that many known filters, such as the Kalman filter [Kalman, 1960], for avoiding the jitter effect is already implemented and the programmers can just drag the filter's icon to the pipeline and connect it to the input to refine the outcome. Figure 5.4 shows the pipeline defined on the server side. A Rigid Body node specifies the input device (iPhone / laser-pointing device). An Intercept Point node calculates the 2D position on the screen, based on the 6D-data of the selected rigid

---

[3]The Squidy Interaction Library is a free software and is published under the license of LGPL: http://site.squidy-lib.de

body. Furthermore, three corners of each screen are defined in the RoomObject node. Another pipeline runs on the other displays (see figure 5.5 below). There, the intersection point is filtered by the Kalman filter module and sent as the mouse position event to the display.

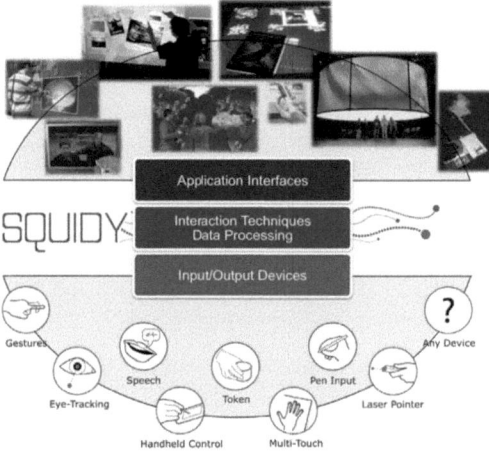

Figure 5.3: Squidy is an interaction library, which offers diverse input modalities. The visual user interface hides the complexity of the technical implementation from the user by providing a simple visual language based on high-level visual data flow programming. Squidy was used in this research to connect the Optitrack system and map the tracking data to the display recognition and mouse movements.

5.5 System Architecture

The system architecture is demonstrated in figure 5.6 below. PrIME (Primitive Interaction tasks for Multi-display Environments) is the name of the project. The position and direction information of the markers is sent to Squidy. The direction of the projection of the input device with the displays is calculated. The intersection point is refined by the Kalman filter and the resulting point is sent as the mouse position event to the corresponding display (that is the display on the

5.5 System Architecture

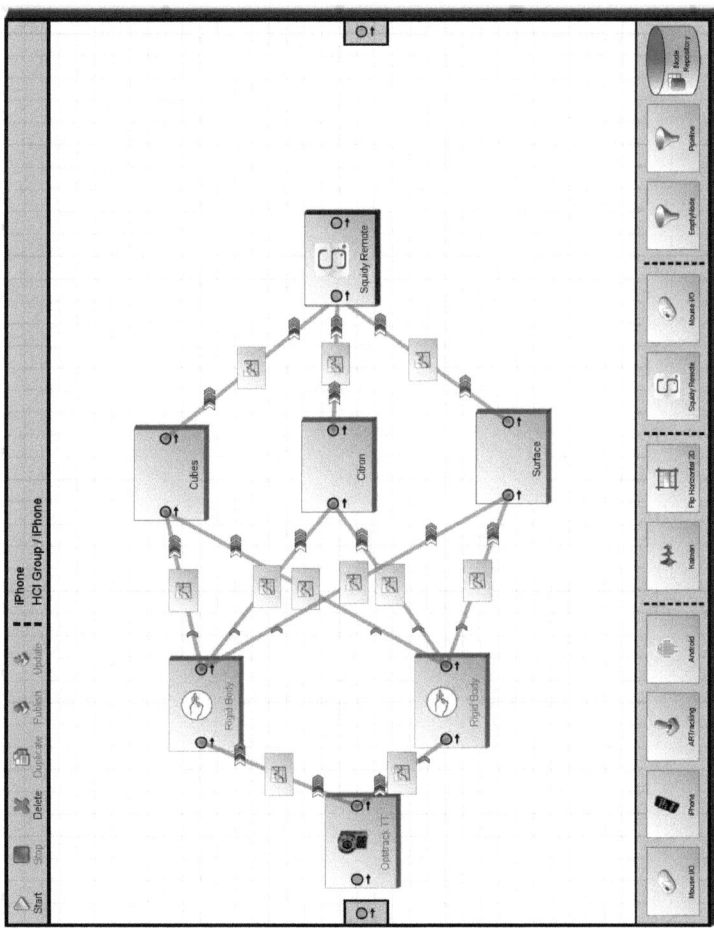

Figure 5.4: The pipeline runs on the server side. It receives the tracking data from the Optitrack system, and sends it to the client displays.

88 5 Methodology

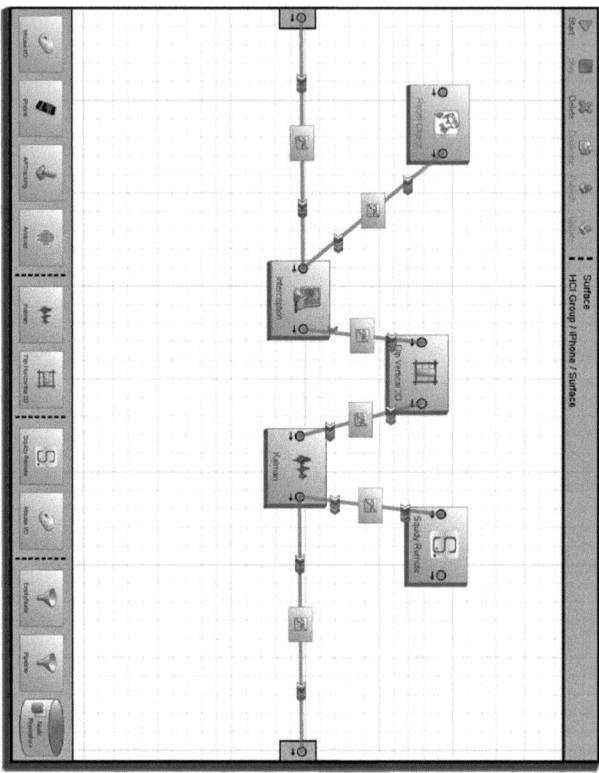

Figure 5.5: The pipeline runs on the Microsoft Surface display. Similar pipeline runs on other display, as well as on the server. For each display the setting of the pipeline has to be adapted, for example the ports. The calculated intersection point is refined by the Kalman filter and is sent as a mouse position event to the client.

focus of the user). By moving the input device, the intersection point is also updated and the result is a smooth movement of the mouse pointer on the displays. This way of pointing is a direct pointing, in contrast with the mouse which uses a relative pointing method. The GUI of the displays is a landscape of objects using the ZOIL Framework, which was implemented at

Human-Computer Interaction working group by Christian Jetter (see more details in [Gerken et al., 2011; Jetter et al., 2008]) and is downloadable as an open-source framework[4].

The iPhone is connected to displays wirelessly. The message exchange between the iPhone and displays is done with OSC and UDP protocols. OSC (Open Sound Protocol) is a framework for sending messages to different multimedia devices. UDP (User Datagram Protocol) is a network protocol, originally used for sending voice data. The server sends the images to the iPhone via the TCP protocol. TCP (Transmission Control Protocol) is one of the core protocols of the Internet Protocol Suite.

While users move the iPhone, they see the visual feedback of the cursor on the display. By achieving the mouse event, the client display sends all the objects as small thumbnails to the iPhone, which in turn shows the images on its small screen, and enables users to select an object by tapping on its thumbnail. The ZOIL framework facilitated this research with a synchronization of data between the displays. One large landscape was defined that includes all of the objects shown on all three displays. Each display is an area (window) of one part of the landscape, that is, it can present just the objects located on that part of the display. This simplified the implementation of the object transfer between the displays by updating the position of the object inside the landscape.

5.6 Experimental Approach

A controlled experiment was carried out to answer the research question. This experiment with a within-subject design approach compared the two selected input devices (the iPhone and the laser-pointing device) by giving the participants pre-defined tasks to perform with both devices. More details about the design of the experiment are presented in chapter 6. The qualitative results were analyzed using the Paired Samples T test, as well as the Wilcoxon Matched-Pair test. The quantitative data were analyzed utilizing the repeated-measure ANOVA test, as well

---

[4]http://zoil.codeplex.com

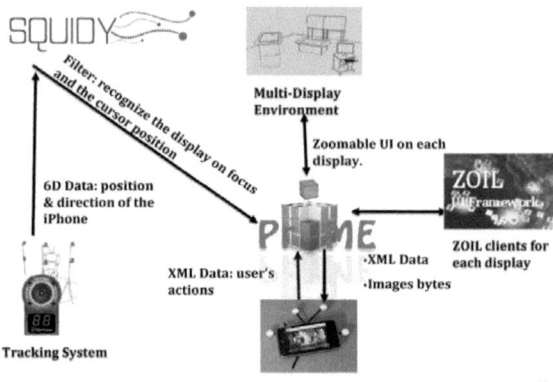

Figure 5.6: System architecture: Optitrack system sends the position and direction data to Squidy ([Rädle, 2010; König, 2010; König et al., 2010]). In Squidy, the intersection point is calculated and this is mapped to the current mouse position on the display, on which the user is currently focusing.

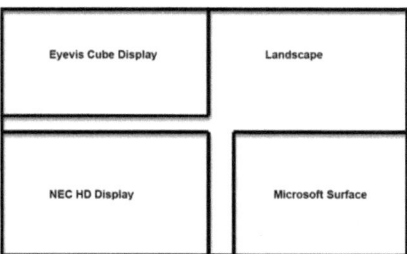

Figure 5.7: This figure demonstrates the space distribution of the landscape between the three displays.

as Mauchly's test and multivariate test (please see [Field, 2009; Jonathan Lazar, 2009] for more information about the statistical methods).

5.7 Summary of the Chapter

This chapter explained the methodology behind this research. The steps which were taken to answer the research question were highlighted in the first part of this chapter. This was followed by a discussion on the potential input devices for MDEs together with their advantages and disadvantages. The third section then, explained the mechanism used to recognize the display on which the user was focusing via the Optitrack system. Finally, the last section dealt with the system infrastructure and architecture.

In the following chapter, the design process of the PrIME project, which is an example prototype for a MDE, is presented.

Input Devices	Advantages	Disadvantages
Mouse & Keyboard	Known	Stationary
	Fast & accurate	
Laser Pointer	Mobile	Public feedback
	Fast for simple tasks	Slow for ordered-based tasks
	Blind interaction	
Digital Pen	Known metaphor	No remote input
	Direct input device	Public feedback
Free Hand Gestures	Mobile	Public feedback
	Remote	High cognitive load
	Compatible	(memorizing gestures)
	Blind interaction	
	No extra input device needed	
Mobile Phone	Mobile	Different platforms
	Remote	Divided focus
	Additional display	
	Individual feedback/info	
	Good for complex tasks	

Table 5.1: The above table compares potential input devices for multi-display environments.

Chapter 6

Multi-Display Interaction: PrIME Project

"I never perfected an invention that I did not think about in terms of the service it might give others."

—Thomas Edison

6.1 Introduction

The theoretical part of the PrIME project (Primitive Interaction tasks for Multi-display Environments) was presented in Chapter 3. This chapter highlights the practical part of the project, which aims to answer the research question:

Does a mobile input device with an integrated display improve performing cross-display interaction tasks?

As was explained in chapter 5, the idea behind this research was to compare two devices, one of which has an integrated display whereas the other does not. The following section highlights the interaction design rational for the iPhone in pointing and object selection tasks.

6.2 iPhone Interaction Design

Pointing is one of the first actions users perform, as they start to interact with a display. In the PrIME prototype, pointing means moving the iPhone to the direction of the display. Moving the device to the left or right, up or down moves the cursor respectively. In this prototype, iPhone is an absolute pointing device. While the user points to a display, the objects of that display are shown on the screen of the iPhone as small thumbnails. Selecting the object is simply done by tapping on the object's thumbnail (see figure 6.1 below).

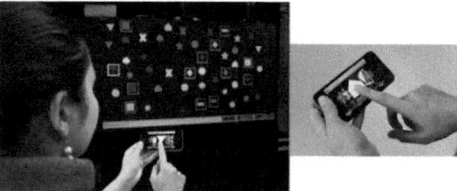

Figure 6.1: The user is selecting the objects on the large display by tapping on the objects on the iPhone. The GUI of the iPhone is designed based on the CoverFlow visualization.

The limited space on the iPhone screen does not allow to show a high number of objects. However, visualization methods such as CoverFlow, or ZoomGrid facilitate more space by scrolling and zooming features. There are several methods for selecting objects on the screen. For example, with the standard keyboard and mouse, users can select an object with a mouse click. Dragging the mouse on the display and drawing a rectangle, thus creating a selection window, enables users to select more objects. Another method is the combination of the shift button and a mouse click (shift + Click). PrIME prototype uses shift + Click function on the iPhone to select objects. The reason for this is that the selection window mechanisms are less handy for the small screen of the iPhone, and thus it takes more time to draw a rectangle with finger gestures than to tap on the screen (see figure 6.2 below). One tap selects an object, and a second tap deselects it. There are three different potential user interfaces for iPhone. A CoverFlow visualization, a zoomable grid (ZoomGrid) visualization and the DisplayMap. More details about each of them are explained

6.2 iPhone Interaction Design

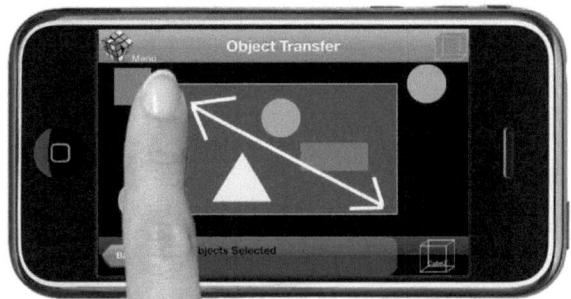

Figure 6.2: This figure illustrates the selection window method for selecting more than one object at once. This method is not so handy for the small screen of the iPhone, and thus it takes more time to draw a rectangle with finger gestures than to tap on the screen.

below.

6.2.1 CoverFlow Visualization

As shown in figure 6.1 above, the objects on the large display are shown in one row as a standard CoverFlow visualization in iPhone. Swiping the finger to the right shows further objects. Tapping on an object selects the object and a second tap deselects it. The number of selected objects is shown at the bottom of the screen.

6.2.2 DisplayMap Visualization

In this visualization, objects are shown exactly the same as on the large display, but in smaller sizes. The screen of the iPhone is the down-scaled version of the large display. In this case, the spatial positions of the objects are the same. For instance the object on the top left, remains on the top left side of the screen (see figure 6.3 below). Selecting an object works the same as in CoverFlow per simple tap. Users can zoom in and out with a standard pinching gesture.

Figure 6.3: The user is selecting the objects on the large display by tapping on the objects on the iPhone. The GUI of the iPhone is based on a DisplayMap visualization. The picture on the top right side illustrates how the GUI looks like when it is zoomed in.

6.2.3 ZoomGrid Visualization

ZoomGrid places the objects inside a 2D grid. Users can zoom in and out with a pinching gesture. Sliding up or down, left or right shows further objects on the screen (see figure 6.4 below). As with the other procedures mentioned earlier, selecting an object can be done with a simple tap.

Figure 6.4: The user is selecting the objects on the large display by tapping on the objects on the iPhone. The GUI of the iPhone is based on a ZoomGrid visualization. The picture on the top right side illustrates how the GUI looks like when it is zoomed in.

6.2.4 Comparison between the GUIs

The three GUI alternatives explained above, have advantages and disadvantages. These were compared in table 6.1 below. The question is, which GUI is preferable for the users in practice? Furthermore, with which GUI can users select objects faster and with less error? The first user study in section 6.3 compares these three GUIs to answer such questions. CoverFlow visualization presents objects bigger than DisplayMap and ZoomGrid. However, objects can be shown bigger in size, by zooming in to them, to a relatively flexible size in both the DisplayMap and the ZoomGrid techniques. In the worst case, selecting an object from CoverFlow takes longer than in the other two techniques, since in N objects, selecting the object number N needs N-1 time swiping, while in the ZoomGrid and the DisplayMap all the user has to do is to scroll the page, or if necessary, zoom in to an object to select. DisplayMap takes a 1-1 mapping from the large display to the iPhone screen, whereas when using the other two techniques the objects' locations are not guaranteed.

Comparison between the GUIs

Apart from the GUI alternatives, another question arises regarding the best ordering of objects. Answers to this question are explored in more details in the following section.

6.2.5 Object Ordering Algorithms

Besides different possibilities for iPhone GUI, it is also a challenge to decide how to put the objects in order. The 2D positions of objects on the large display is available. How should this be mapped to a 1D position in a CoverFlow visualization? The answer is also not trivial for ZoomGrid, since some objects may not fit in their original row and thus have to be shifted down. DisplayMap shows the exact order without any changes. Therefore, it has just one possibility to put the objects in order. Three potential ordering algorithms for CoverFlow and ZoomGrid are considered, namely, Left to Right, Z-Order Curve and Hilbert Curve for Coverflow, and Left to Right, PixelMap Density and PixelMap Left to Right for ZoomGrid.

GUI Type	Pros	Cons
CoverFlow	• Bigger images and thus more recognizable for users. • Standard in iPhones.	At a glance, the user can only see 9 images. Moreover, to select objects, the user might have to swipe over several images.
ZoomGrid	• On average, quicker selection of objects, since 48 objects are visible at once. • Zooming can enlarge the objects.	The user has to concentrate more to find the mapping between two displays.
DisplayMap	• Consistency between the two displays. • Zooming can enlarge objects on demand.	• Selecting overlapped objects is difficult. • The empty space between object remains unused. • For scattered objects, the user needs to scroll more than in ZoomGrid.

Table 6.1: This table lists the advantages and disadvantages of CoverFlow, ZoomGrid, and DisplayMap GUIs.

CoverFlow Ordering Approaches

The three algorithms which were considered to put the objects on CoverFlow visualization in order are:

- Left to Right:
  The first possibility is the left-to-right and the top-to-bottom order, just as people read books in English.

- Z-Order Curve [Morton, 1996; Orenstein and Merrett, 1984]:
  It is a space-filling curve which maps multidimensional data to one dimension while preserving the locality of the data points (see figure 6.5 below). This approach suggests that people sometimes try to read from left to right but still accomplish the left area first and then continue to the other area on the right.

Figure 6.5: Z-Order Curve illustrated for four iterations.

- Hilbert Curve [Faloutsos and Roseman, 1989; Arvo, 1991]:
  It is a continuous factorial space-filling curve, which fills a square. Every point in the square is visited with a size of

  $$2 \times 2, 4 \times 4, 8 \times 8, 16 \times 16, etc. (any power of 2).$$

The basic element for the Hilbert Curve is a square with an open side. This square defines the first order (see figure 6.6 below). The second order replaces one square with four

Figure 6.6: Hilbert Curve first order.

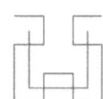

Figure 6.7: Hilbert Curve's second order. The square with one open side from the first order is replaced by 4 smaller ones and 3 join vectors.

smaller ones that are joined with 3 vectors (see figure 6.7 below).

Next orders repeat this process by replacing one square by four smaller ones with 3 vectors joining them.

The Hilbert Curve is applied in image processing, especially in image compression. This approach shows its advantages where the coherence [1] between neighboring pixels is important. In this research, this approach is applied to check whether it is beneficial for the problem.

ZoomGrid Visualization

The following three algorithms are considered for putting objects in order on the ZoomGrid visualization:

- Left to Right:
  It is the same approach as the one used for the CoverFlow, that is, sorting the objects from left to right and from top to bottom.

- PixelMap: Density
  PixelMap is a visual data mining approach described in [Keim et al., 2003]. This algorithm suggests the mapping of a big data set in such a way that:

    1. no data points overlap each other (no overlap constraint).

---

[1]The coherence level is the amount in which neighboring pixels are at sequential positions on the space filling curve.

6.2 iPhone Interaction Design

2. the new positions should be as close as possible to the original positions (position preservation constraint).
3. the data points that have similarity, that means are in the same cluster, should be positioned close to each other (Clustering Constraint).

This algorithm is presented to solve optimization problems, such as displaying the data set related to purchases with a credit card. This data set is stored with the related geo-spatial data. It is useful to relate the parameters and to detect local correlations, dependencies, and other interesting patterns.

The PrIME ordering problem can be mapped to the properties of the PixelMap algorithm. Instead of pixels, PrIME deals with the objects on the display. The object mapping on the iPhone should include no overlapping between the objects. Furthermore, the location of the object should be as close as possible to the original location. These constraints match the constraints of the PixelMap algorithm. However, the clustering constraint is not applicable, since the objects do not have any relationship to each other.

PixelMap applies to the set of object positions on the display as follows. The number of regions inside the grid is equal to or greater than the number of objects on the display. The algorithm then takes the sizes and the positions of the objects on the large display and after that it generates the grid with the calculated regions. The next step would be for each object to be mapped to a free region with the smallest Euclidian distance. The objects are repeatedly divided in half. This division alternates between the x- and y-axis. The order in which the objects are mapped is very important as it can significantly change the resulting mappings. In this case, the algorithm continues, starting with the half that has a higher density, that is a higher number of objects.

The output of the algorithm is the mapping of the objects into the regions of the grid. This is then presented on the iPhone screen (see figure 6.9 below).

- PixelMap: Left to Right
  With regard to this research, another variety of the PixelMap algorithm is defined by a combination of the two

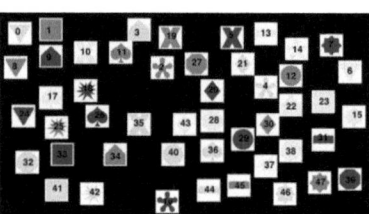

Figure 6.8: This figure shows the result of applying the PixelMap Density approach on the objects inside the display.

above approaches, namely: Left to Right and PixelMap density. This algorithm works the same as the PixelMap density, but after dividing the objects in half, it processes the half on the left side first. Therefore, the density factor does not play a role in this algorithm.

Using an iPhone as an input device to control a large display, which GUI and which ordering algorithm would be the fastest and more preferable for the users?
Experiment 1 aimed to answer this research question. The following section reports the results of the experiment.

6.3 Experiment 1: GUI Battle

There are three different potential user interfaces for the iPhone, namely the CoverFlow visualization, the zoomable grid (ZoomGrid) visualization and the DisplayMap. For each of these visualizations, except for the DisplayMap, different algorithms are used to put objects in order. It is interesting to know which visualization and which algorithm performs best for the users in terms of user acceptance and expectations, as well as interaction speed. Therefore, a user study to compare these techniques was carried out, which is presented in the next section.

6.3 Experiment 1: GUI Battle

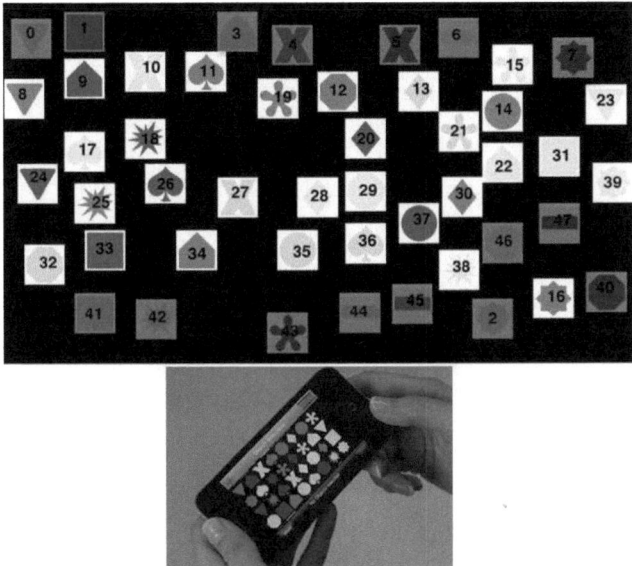

Figure 6.9: This figure shows the result of applying the PixelMap Left To Right approach on the objects inside the display. On the iPhone the objects with ordering from 8 to 39 are shown.

6.3.1 Experiment Design

A within-subject experiment design was used in this research. 16 users were tested, 8 of whom were men and 8 were women (18-55 years old). Each user tested seven different conditions (DisplayMap + 3 * CoverFlow + 3* ZoomGrid). The hypothesis was that DisplayMap would be faster than ZoomGrid UI and CoverFlow would be the slowest in selecting objects. The reason for this assumption was that DisplayMap provides an overview of the objects in the same relative locations as they are distributed on the large display. Therefore, the user would need less time to map the real objects with their thumbnails on the iPhone. CoverFlow was assumed to be the slowest, since in the worst case for n objects the user needs to swipe n - 1 times to get to the right object. The other two visualizations show the objects in one glance.

The dependent variables were selection speed, accuracy, task accomplishment (success) rate and user satisfaction. Furthermore, the independent variables were the 3 different GUIs for iPhone mentioned earlier, namely CoverFlow, ZoomGrid, DisplayMap as well as other different object-ordering techniques for each visualization. Users filled in a questionnaire, which included questions about the users' background experience, as well as their impression and preferences of the techniques used. The clicks on the server side were timed and videos were taken for further analyses.

In order to answer the research question as to which GUI performs best, one large vertical HD display was used (see figure 6.10 below). In the beginning, the moderator clarified the way of interaction to the user and let the user play around with the device till he or she felt comfortable with it. Afterwards, the actual task commenced and the user's interaction was recorded in a log file. The task was to select the objects, which were highlighted in red on the large display, on the iPhone. Through this task the user was led to look at the large display and find the predefined objects on the iPhone. The user repeated the task using seven different conditions. For all the seven conditions, 48 objects were shown on the display. After completing this task, he or she was asked to fill in a questionnaire about background experience and impressions and preferences regarding the three GUIs. The user's interaction (time of selection) was logged and his or her behavior was recorded on video.

6.3.2 Results

The task completion time means and standard deviations for the 7 different techniques are illustrated in tables 6.2, 6.3 and 6.4 below. Log files show that the quickest method for 9 users was the ZoomGrid with the PixelMap Left-to-Right approach.

The repeated measures ANOVA test was applied to compare the means of task completion time, coverage rate and error rate. The error rate was measured through the number of deselections and selections of wrong objects. The coverage rate is the ratio of the number of correct selections to the whole number of selections

6.3 Experiment 1: GUI Battle

Figure 6.10: The user is selecting objects from the vertical Eyevis Cube display.

GUI: CoverFlow	Left to Right	Hilbert	Z-Order
Mean	65.06 s	58.25 s	48.27 s
Standard Deviation	38.10 s	38.48 s	20.20 s

Table 6.2: This table lists the means and standard deviations of the task completion time for three different ordering algorithms with CoverFlow visualization.

GUI: ZoomGrid	PixelMap: Left to Right	PixelMap: Density	Left-to-Right
Mean	20.56 s	25.12 s	22.44 s
Standard Deviation	11.78 s	12.48 s	11.23 s

Table 6.3: This table lists the means and standard deviations of the task completion time for three different ordering algorithms with ZoomGrid visualization.

GUI Type	DisplayMap	ZoomGrid AVG	CoverFlow AVG
Mean	22.20 s	23.33 s	53.20 s
Standard Deviation	9.41 s	10.83 s	18.82 s

Table 6.4: This table lists the mean and standard deviations of the task completion time for the DisplayMap, CoverFlow and ZoomGrid GUI. The type of ordering algorithm is ignored here, therefore, the average of the values for different algorithms are considered for each type of GUI.

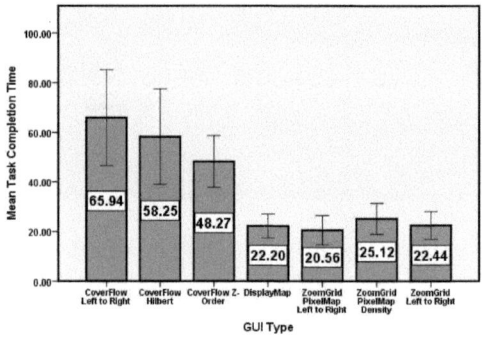

Figure 6.11: This diagram shows the mean task completion time for all the 7 GUIs. It indicates that the fastest GUI is the ZoomGrid PixelMap Left to Right. Two other GUIs, namely, the DisplayMap and ZoomGrid Left to Right are slightly different than the ZoomGrid PixelMap Left to Right.

of all 12 objects. To compare the means of the three GUI types, regardless of the ordering algorithm, the average value between the three ordering algorithms were taken. This value is called CoverFlow AVG and ZoomGrid AVG (see table 6.4 above). The CoverFlow AVG (M = 53.20, SD= 18.82) was slower than the other two GUI types (DisplayMap, M= 22.20, SD=9.41 and ZoomGrid AVG, M=23.33, SD=10.83). The result showed a significant main effect on the task completion time for the GUI type ($F(2, 28) = 39.360, p = 0.000, \alpha = 0.05$). Tests of within-subject contrast indicate that CoverFlow AVG is significantly slower than the ZoomGrid AVG (($F(1, 14) = 41.593 p = 0.000, \alpha = 0.05$), and DisplayMap ($F(1, 14) = 57.627, p = 0.000, \alpha = 0.05$). The

6.3 Experiment 1: GUI Battle

GUI Type	DisplayMap	ZoomGrid AVG	CoverFlow AVG
Mean	1.19	0.85	1.47
Standard Deviation	2.713	0.834	0.976

Table 6.5: This table lists the mean and standard deviations of the error rate in the DisplayMap, CoverFlow and ZoomGrid GUI as the number of errors. The type of ordering algorithm was ignored here, therefore, the average of the values for different algorithms were considered for each GUI type.

GUI: CoverFlow	Left to Right	Hilbert	Z-Order
Mean	1.69	1.25	1.40
Standard Deviation	1.621	0.931	2.028

Table 6.6: This table lists the means and standard deviations of the error rate for three different ordering algorithms with the CoverFlow visualization as the number of errors.

difference between the ZoomGrid AVG and DisplayMap was not significant ($F(1, 14) = 0.143, p = 0.711, \alpha = 0.05$).

The means and standard deviations in error- and coverage rate for the seven GUIs are listed in tables 6.5, 6.6, 6.7, 6.8, 6.9, 6.10 below. They are also illustrated in diagrams 6.12 and 6.13 below. The ZoomGrid PixelMap Left to Right GUI has a lower error rate but a higher coverage rate in average.

Mauchly's test showed that the assumption of sphericity is violated to compare the means of the error rate ($\chi^2(2) = 21.873, p = 0.000, \alpha = 0.05$). Therefore, the multivariate test is applied ($\epsilon = 0.58$). The means of the error rate for different GUIs is not significant, since $V = 0.29, F(2, 14) = 2.859, P = 0.91, \alpha = 0.05$.

A similar result was achieved for the coverage rate of the GUIs. Therefore, Mauchly's test indicates that the sphericity is violated ($\chi^2(2) = 17.238, p = 0.000 < 0.05$). The multivariate test showed that the type of GUI affects the coverage rate ($V = 0.44, F(2, 14) = 5.522, p = 0.017, \alpha = 0.05$).

A final interview with the participants showed that 10 users preferred the ZoomGrid whereas 6 preferred the DisplayMap.

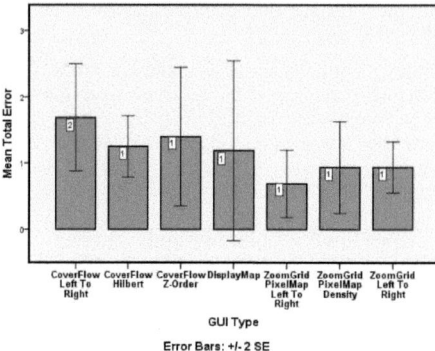

Figure 6.12: The above diagram shows the mean error rate for all the 7 GUIs. The error rate was measured through the number of deselections and selections of wrong objects.

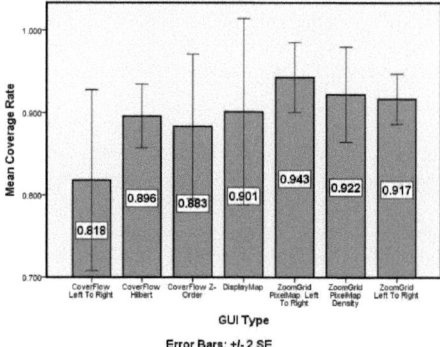

Figure 6.13: This diagram shows the mean coverage rate for all the 7 GUIs. It shows that the ZoomGrid PixelMap Left to Right GUI is slightly higher in the coverage ratio (the range is from 0 to 1, where 1 means 100% of the task was completed).

6.3 Experiment 1: GUI Battle

GUI: ZoomGrid	PixelMap: Left to Right	PixelMap: Density	Left-to-Right
Mean	0.69	0.94	0.94
Standard Deviation	1.014	1.389	0.772

Table 6.7: This table lists the means and standard deviations of the error rate for three different ordering algorithms with the ZoomGrid visualization as the number of errors.

GUI Type	DisplayMap	ZoomGrid AVG	CoverFlow AVG
Mean	0.901	0.927	0.864
Standard Deviation	0.23	0.069	0.101

Table 6.8: This table lists the mean and standard deviations of the coverage rate in the DisplayMap, CoverFlow and ZoomGrid GUI (the range is from 0 to 1, where 1 means 100% of the task was completed). The type of ordering algorithm is ignored here, therefore, the average of the values for different algorithms are considered for each GUI type.

6.3.3 Discussion

The results indicate that CoverFlow is too slow for this type of task.

Although it was assumed that DisplayMap would be the fastest and most preferable technique, results show that most of the users preferred ZoomGrid. One of the reasons mentioned in the questionnaires was that ZoomGrid gives them a clearer overview of the existing objects. Another reason was that the object presentation on ZoomGrid was bigger than on DisplayMap.

Although the users practiced zooming to enlarge objects with two fingers, they preferred avoiding this action during the task. They

GUI: CoverFlow	Left to Right	Hilbert	Z-Order
Mean	0.818	0.896	0.883
Standard Deviation	0.220	0.078	0.170

Table 6.9: This table lists the means and standard deviations of the coverage rate for three different ordering algorithms with the CoverFlow visualization (the range is from 0 to 1, where 1 means 100% of the task was completed).

GUI: ZoomGrid	PixelMap: Left to Right	PixelMap: Density	Left to Right
Mean	0.943	0.922	0.917
Standard Deviation	0.085	0.115	0.061

Table 6.10: This table lists the means and standard deviations of the coverage rate for three different ordering algorithms with the ZoomGrid visualization (the range is from 0 to 1, where 1 means 100% of the task was completed).

believed that zooming was one of the failures of the GUI as the latter did not present big enough objects and so they had to zoom in to be able to select an object.

CoverFlow was not preferred by the users. They thought it was slow when it came to selecting objects, and also that one could only see 9 objects at a glance. In addition, only the object located in the middle of the view is selectable per tap, which means that the user had to swipe further to select other objects.

The within-subject design of the experiment let all the users try all the conditions. An advantage of this was that the users were able to compare the techniques. On the other hand, one disadvantage which was noticed was that the users were not willing to use the zoom option and expected the objects on the display to be big enough for them to see. This happened when they were using CoverFlow and ZoomGrid, but not when using the DisplayMap GUI. The users' opinion might have been different, if the experiment had used a between-subject design approach.

The maximum number of objects on the display in both experiments was 48. For more objects to be added, other techniques would had to be applied for scalability, which is discussed in section 6.7.5.

As the result of the experiment showed, CoverFlow visualization is significantly slower than the other two GUIs, therefore, it is not appropriate for these sort of tasks. DisplayMap and ZoomGrid were both similarly fast. In fact no significant difference was indicated. According to the subjective feedback by the users, the ZoomGrid GUI was preferable, because it showed a good overview of the existing objects. Furthermore, from an interaction designer's point of view, the ZoomGrid has an advantage of using the whole space available on the iPhone screen for presenting the objects. This contrasts to DisplayMap that maps the empty space between the objects from the large display to the iPhone screen. Therefore, users had to slide or scroll less often, and could see a higher number of objects at one glance. ZoomGrid also showed good results regarding the error and coverage rate when compared to the other six GUIs. This leaded to the decision of choosing the ZoomGrid PixelMap Left to Right method for the iPhone.

6.4 Bridging the Gap between Displays

In a single-display setting, the graphical representation of the cursor gives users feedback about the current position of the cursor. While moving an object inside the display, the user can always see the visual representation of that object. On the other hand, in multi-display settings, different screens are located physically apart from each other. When the pointer is moved from one display to another, it disappears between the display physical spaces. The idea is to use an iPhone as an input device to transfer objects or to move the cursor from one display to another. This advantage of the mobile phone is also considered by other researchers such as Boring et al. [2010].

After selecting the objects of interest, these are visually shown on the iPhone. Therefore, selected objects move with the user around the room until the user performs the drop action. By presenting the icon of that display, the iPhone screen shows which display is currently in focus. Therefore, the paste action is done by tapping on the icon of the target display. The new objects will directly be added to the former objects on the target display. The iPhone acts as a clipboard and stores the selected objects in its Selected Object view (see figure 6.14 below). The objects selected from different displays are presented with a colored frame corresponding to that display. For example, the objects selected from the Microsoft Surface have a red frame. Clicking the tab of any display would filter the objects from that display (see figure 6.15 below).

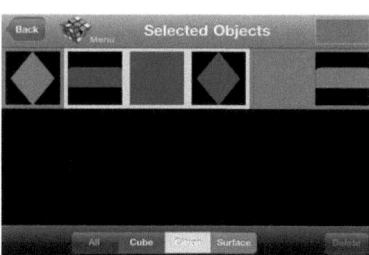

Figure 6.14: A screen shot of an iPhone clipboard view. The objects with a green frame are selected from the citron display whereas the red ones are selected from the Microsoft Surface.

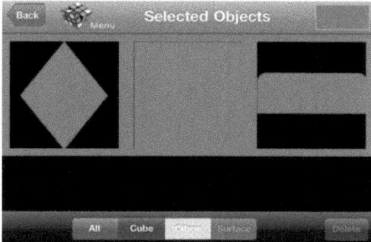

Figure 6.15: As the user clicked on the 'Surface' tab, the objects that are selected from this display are filtered with the color of the corresponding display (here the red color).

As can be seen in figure 6.16 below, on the top left side of the screen, there is a menu button. This screen shows the actions, for example object transfer.

As mentioned earlier in chapter 5, a laser-pointing device represents a remote input device without a display. The following section highlights the decisions taken regarding design.

6.5 Laser-pointing Device Interaction Design

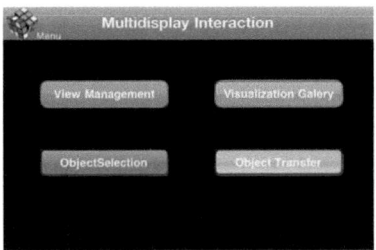

Figure 6.16: A screenshot of the iphone, on the top left side of the screen, there is a menu button. This screen shows the available actions, for example object transfer.

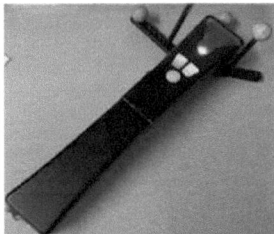

Figure 6.17: This figure shows the laser-pointing device. It has three buttons for selecting an object, opening a right-click menu, and start saving log files for user studies.

6.5 Laser-pointing Device Interaction Design

Werner König developed a laser pointer at the Human-Computer Interaction group of the University of Konstanz. As can be seen in figure 6.17 above, this device has three buttons. It is meant for interacting with a single display and its original functionality is through infrared camera, which is usually located at the back of the display. However, for the PrIME experiment, another mechanism was used for pointing, namely the OptiTrack tracking system, which was also used for the iPhone. The reason behind this was to fix the pointing-mechanism variable to give a fair comparison of both devices in the second experiment (explained in section 6.7).

The user points to an object and clicks on the top left button in order to select it. The top right button then, opened a menu for the user to select an action (see figure 6.18 below), for example, object transfer. The third rounded button is used to start or else to stop at the beginning and at the end of the experiment tasks. The system records the user's behavior in log files. Meanwhile, the rounded button is activated. The user can transfer one or more

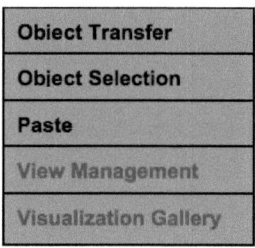

Figure 6.18: This figure shows the right-click menu that opens when users click on the second button on the laser-pointing device. There, the user can select an action, for example object transfer. The last two items were disabled since they were not included in the experiment.

objects from one display to another by first pointing to the objects of interest, clicking the left button to select, second clicking the right button and then select the item "object transfer" from the pop-up menu. The user then turns to the target display, points somewhere on the display and select the item "paste" from the right click menu.

Other possibilities exist in order to transfer objects to another display using the laser-pointing device. One of these is the well-known technique of dragging the objects across displays. This technique was not chosen in this research for two main reasons. First, the displays inside the room might be positioned at a few meters distance from each other, which means that the user would have to push the selection button through the whole room till he or she points to the next display. This could be on the one hand tiring for the user and on the other hand could be more error-prone with distance, since users might drop the objects by accidentally releasing the button at the wrong position [Rekimoto, 1997]. Second, for the iPhone's interaction technique, it was not necessary to press buttons for long stretches of time. Therefore, it would be inaccurate to compare the iPhone with the laser-pointing device, as they are using completely different object-transfer mechanisms.

6.6 The iPhone vs. the Laser-Pointing Device

Before running the experiment, it was expected that the iPhone would perform better than the laser-pointing device in situations such as the following.

1. Selecting small objects. This is because with the laser-pointing device, the user would have to move closer to the display to recognize the object, whereas with the iPhone the objects are visible on its screen. The same situation can be considered when the displays are at a distance or when the room is crowded and some people are standing in front of the large display. In such a situation, the integrated display of the iPhone can give the user the visual feedback and the possibility to continue the interaction.

2. Selecting overlapping objects. They can be recognized much easier and can be selected faster with the iPhone, since the laser-pointing device has to drag all the above objects aside in order to be able to find and select the object beneath it. On the other hand, the iPhone shows all the objects next to each other without considering the overlapping issues.

3. Performing complex ordered-based tasks, such as transferring objects from multiple displays to other multiple displays using ordered-based tasks. This would be quicker using the iPhone, since all the objects can first be collected (clipboard functionality) and then distributed to the target displays. On the other hand, with the laser pointer only an N to 1 display object-transfer is possible. This means that several objects can be selected from multiple displays, but they can only be pasted on one display.

The following are predictions as to where the laser-pointing device would perform better than the iPhone.

1. Selecting big-sized objects (i.e. objects that are recognizable for the users from their current distance to the display).

2. Performing simple tasks, such as transferring one object from a display to another, given that the users do not continuously have to concentrate on and shift their focus between two displays.

One main difference between the iPhone and the laser-pointing device is that for the iPhone the user interface is distributed between the large display and the iPhone screen. This needs continues switching between these two displays, which is also called divided attention. This can lead to higher cognitive load and make the task completion slower that the laser-pointing device. The following section describes the comparison experiment between the iPhone and the laser-pointing device.

6.7 Experiment 2: Input Devices Battle

6.7.1 Experiment Design

The aim of this experiment was to compare the iPhone to the laser-pointing device as two alternative interaction devices in multi-display environments. The iPhone represents devices with an integrated display whereas the laser-pointing device represents devices without a display. The first experiment helped to select a proper GUI type for the iPhone, namely the *ZoomGrid* with the *PixelMap Left to Right* ordering approach.

The experiment included a within-subject experiment design. The hypothesis was that the iPhone performs better than the laser-pointing device in accomplishing multi-display selection and object-transfer tasks. In this experiment the independent variable was the input device, (that is, the iPhone or the laser-pointing device), whereas the dependent variables were the users' performance and satisfaction. 18 users (9 men and 9 women, 19-36 years old) participated. As in the previous experiment, evaluation log files were stored and the users' behaviour was recorded on video.

6.7 Experiment 2: Input Devices Battle

The concrete Hypotheses were as follows.

Concrete Hypothesis:

Hypothesis 1: The iPhone is faster than the laser-pointing device for selecting objects that are not recognizable from the user's current position (since they are too small, or the distance between the user and the display is too far.)
Expectation: It is assumed that users have to get closer to the display, in order to be able to recognize the objects and select them with the laser-pointing device. The iPhone provides an overview of the objects as a thumbnail, therefore the distance to the original display, as well as the sizes of the objects on the large display does not play a role in the interaction.
Independent variables: Input device (iPhone, laser-pointing device), object size (small, big).
Dependent variables: Interaction speed, user satisfaction
Task: Two large vertical displays were used and were positioned close to each other (see figure 6.20 below). Some images of animals as well as texts with the names of animals were distributed on two displays. The user's task was to select a specific animal which the moderator mentions in the beginning, as image and text on both displays. All the users repeated this task with the laser-pointing device and with the iPhone, as well as with big- and small-sized objects.

Hypothesis 2: The iPhone is faster than the laser-pointing device for transferring multiple objects from multiple displays to multiple displays (order-based tasks).
Expectation: It is expected that iPhone performs better than the laser-pointing device for more complex tasks, since the clipboard of the iPhone can memorize the selected objects from each display and this can accelerate the object transfer process.
Independent variables: Input device (iPhone, laser-pointing device)
Dependent variables: Interaction speed, user satisfaction
Task:

1. The user selected one object (blue X) from display 1 and transferred it to display 2 (see figure 6.21 below).

2. The user selected the shapes that include four edges from display 1, and pasted the blue ones in display 2 (3 objects)

and the red ones (3 objects) in display 3. The objects were abstract shapes with different colors (see figure 6.19 below).

Hypothesis 3: The iPhone is faster in selecting objects hidden behind other objects (overlapping landscape)
Expectation: The iPhone shows all the objects without overlapping. But the laser-pointing device can not help finding those objects. Therefore, the user might have to move the objects positioned above, in order to see the hidden ones. Independent variables: Input device (iPhone, laser-pointing device)
Dependent variables: Interaction speed, user satisfaction
Task: The user had to select red and yellow triangles. 2 objects had to be selected but another 4 objects were hidden behind other objects, so that the user had to drag objects aside in order to recognize if they were triangles or not (see figure 6.22 above).

Figure 6.19: The user is transferring objects from the vertical display in the middle to the other two displays using the iPhone.

Each user tested 5 different conditions, as mentioned above, namely, H1-small object, H1-Big object, H2-one object transfer, H2-multiple object transfer, H3-overlapping objects.

Prior to taking part in this research, the users' eyesight were tested. This was necessary in order to make sure that all the users were able to accomplish the task with small objects. The users started with H3 (overlapping objects), where only

6.7 Experiment 2: Input Devices Battle

Figure 6.20: The user is selecting objects with the iPhone. The objects consist of pictures of animals or text with the names of the animals.

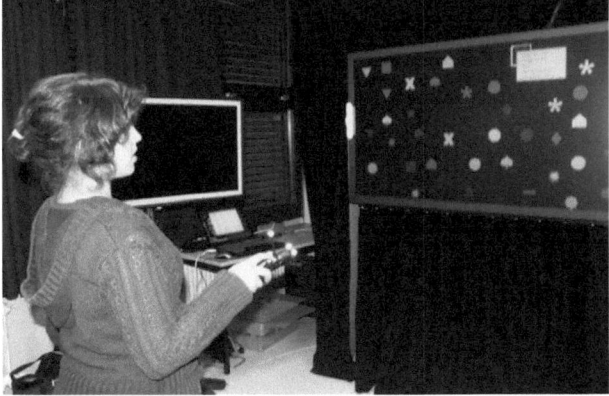

Figure 6.21: The user is transferring one object from one display to another using the laser-pointing device.

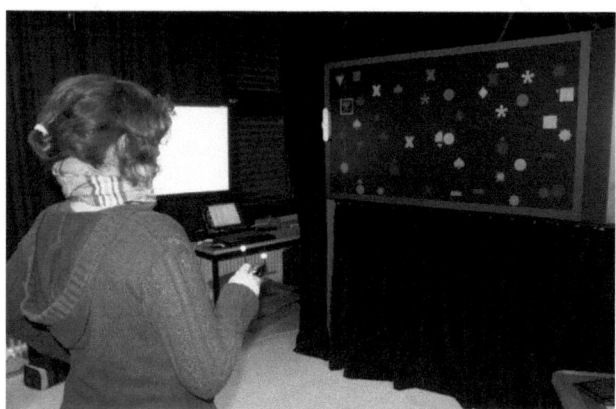

Figure 6.22: The user is selecting objects with the laser-pointing device. The objects could be overlapping or hidden behind other objects.

one vertical display was needed (see figure 6.22 below). The moderator explained how the interaction technique worked and the users had the opportunity to test the device, till they felt comfortable with it. They then started the actual task, once with the laser-pointing device and another time with the iPhone. Half the users first used the iPhone whereas others used the laser-pointing device first.

The users then continued with the H1 with big (120*120 pixels) and small (60*60 pixels) objects, using two vertical displays (see figure 6.20 above). They followed the same procedure as with the H3, completing the task with the iPhone as well as with the laser-pointing device. Finally, they accomplished the H2 with one object-transfer first (see figure 6.21 above) and then with more object-transfers (see figure 6.19 above). For one object-transfer, just the two vertical displays were used, whereas for more object-transfers all the three large displays were utilized.

In all conditions, users had the time to test the device before performing the task. After each task, users filled in a questionnaire with questions about the problems encountered. They were also asked to compare the two input devices used to perform the task. At the end they got a final questionnaire

6.7   Experiment 2: Input Devices Battle   121

with questions about their background knowledge and also their preference between the iPhone and the laser-pointing device.

Three displays were used to run the experiment in the media room (see figure 6.19 above). These were two large vertical displays and a Microsoft surface as a horizontal display. More detailes about the technical set-up were presented earlier in chapter 5.

6.7.2   Results

The second study compared the laser-pointing device and the iPhone using three large displays. The means and standard deviations for the task completion time is listed in tables 6.2, 6.3 and 6.4.

A Paired Samples T-test with $\alpha = 0.05$ suggested that the iPhone is significantly faster than the laser-pointing device when selecting overlapping objects (t(17)=3.024, p=0.008), small-sized objects on two displays (t(14)=6.430, p=0.000), and when transferring one object from one display to another (t(15)=2.205, p=0.043). No significant difference was found between the laser-pointing device and the iPhone when selecting big-sized objects on two displays (t(13)=1.069, p=0.304), and when transferring multiple objects from one display to two other displays (t(14)=0.446, p=0.663).

The error rate of the laser-pointing device for selecting the small objects was (M=0.80, SD=1.47), whereas for the iPhone it was (M=0.07, SD=0.26). The difference between the error rate of the iPhone and the laser-pointing device was not significant ($t(14) = 1.852, p = 0.085\alpha = 0.05$). The descriptive statistics for the error rate of the laser-pointing device for selecting the big objects was (M=0.07, SD=0.27), and for the iPhone (M=0.71, SD=1.86). The difference between the error rate of the iPhone and the laser-pointing device was also not significant (t(13)=1.262, p=0.229).

All of the users accomplished the object transfer tasks (Hypothesis 2) completely and without any error with both input devices. Selecting overlapping objects was also accomplished

Device	Descriptive Statistics	H1: big	H1: small
iPhone	Mean	35.64 s	25 s
	Standard Deviation	19.09 s	6.99 s
Laser-pointing device	Mean	31.07 s	51 s
	Standard Deviation	12.86 s	11.36 s

Table 6.11: This table lists the mean and standard deviations of the task completion time for the two tasks of the first hypothesis.

Device	Descriptive Statistics	H2: one	H2: more
iPhone	Mean	15 s	54.73 s
	Standard Deviation	9.421 s	20.24 s
Laser-pointing device	Mean	23	52.33
	Standard Deviation	12.35 s	17.12 s

Table 6.12: This table lists the mean and standard deviations of the task completion time for the two tasks of hypothesis two.

completely with both input devices. Comparing the error rates between the two input devices in Hypothesis 3 would not make sense, since the users had to move the objects above the objects of interest to select them. This led to a higher number of clicks for the laser-pointing device than for the iPhone.

6.7.3 Subjective Feedback

At the end of the experiment users filled in a qualitative questionnaire. The questions were divided into two different categories. The first category of questions compared two input devices to each other, for example, which input device was more proper for the task. A scale of 1-7 (1: Laser-pointing device, 4: the same, 7: iPhone) was used. Results were analyzed using the One Sampling T-test with $\alpha = 0.05$. The following three questions were taken from this category. For all of these questions, the

6.7 Experiment 2: Input Devices Battle

Device	Descriptive Statistics	H3: Overlapping
iPhone	Mean	22 s
	Standard Deviation	27.722 s
Laser-pointing device	Mean	55 s
	Standard Deviation	32.766 s

Table 6.13: This table lists the mean and standard deviations of the task completion time for the task of overlapping object, hypothesis three. The standard deviation for iPhone is relatively high. The reason is that one user took much longer to accomplish the task than others. Other users finished the task in less than 29 seconds, but this user took 129 seconds. The backup video shows that the user was confused in the beginning and therefore played around with the device for a while before starting the task.

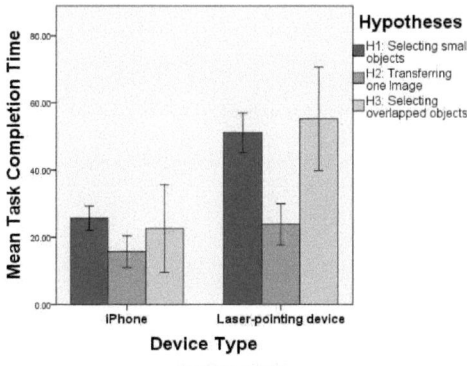

Figure 6.23: The above diagram shows three conditions, where the iPhone was significantly faster, namely when selecting small objects from two displays, when selecting overlapping objects and when transferring one object from a display to another.

iPhone was significantly preferred by the users.

Comparative Questions:

- Which input device was more natural/intuitive? Scale of 1-7 (1: Laser-pointing device, 4: the same, 7: iPhone)

  The majority of users found the iPhone more natural than

the laser-pointing device (T- test significant t(15)=4.371, p=0.001)

- Which input device was better fit for the task? Scale of 1-7 (1: Laser-pointing device, 4: the same, 7: iPhone)

  The majority of users found the iPhone more suitable than the laser-pointing device (T- test significant t(15)=8.295, p=0.000)

- With which input device did you enjoy doing the task most? Scale of 1-7 (1: Laser-pointing device, 4: the same, 7: iPhone)

  The majority of users preferred the iPhone than the laser-pointing device (T- test significant t(16)=3.647, p=0.002)

The second category of questions asked for the users' separate opinion on each input device. For each question a sale of 1-7 was used. The following six questions fell into this category. The results were analyzed using a Paired- Samples T-test with $\alpha = 0.05$. The users' answers for both input devices were compared. The analysis showed that the iPhone was considered significantly better than the laser-pointing device with regard to being easier to use, more accurate for object selection, less tiring to carry (less fatigue) and with regard to the responsiveness to the users input.

Separate questions for usability issues were asked for both input devices as followings.

- Up to what extent did the iPhone distract you from performing the task? Scale of 1-7 (1: Not at all, 7: very distracting)

  The difference variable of distraction for iPhone and laser-pointing device D(16)=0.25, p=0.006, was significantly non-normal.
  No significant difference is between the distraction factor by the iPhone (Mdn=1) and by the laser-pointing device (Mdn=2): z=-1.0679, p=0.093, T=5.

- Up to what extent was the iPhone easy to use? Scale of 1-7 (1: Not easy at all, 7: very easy)

  According to the Paired Samples T-test, the iPhone was significantly easier to control than the laser-pointing device (iPhone: M=6.24 SD=1.091, Laser-pointing device: M=4.41, SD=1.46), t(16)=4.002 p=0.001

- How accurate was the iPhone for selecting objects? Scale of 1-7 (1: very inaccurate, 7: very accurate)

  The difference variable of accuracy for iPhone and laser-pointing device D(16) = 0.23, p=0.027, was significantly non-normal.
  The iPhone is significantly more accurate (Mdn = 7) than the laser-pointing device (Mdn = 4.5): z= -2.810, p = 0.005, T = 14.

- How quick was the reaction of the iPhone to your input? Scale of 1-7 (1: very slow, 7: very quick)

  The difference variable of the responsiveness for iPhone and laser-pointing device D(16) = 0.27, p=0.003, was significantly non-normal.
  The responsiveness of the iPhone is significantly higher (Mdn = 7) than the laser-pointing device (Mdn = 6): z= -2.558, p = 0.011, T = 8.

- How did you like the iPhone? Scale of 1-7 (1: didn't like, 7: like very much)

  According to the Paired Samples T-test, users liked the iPhone significantly more than the laser-pointing device (iPhone: M= 6.13 SD=1.088, Laser-pointing device: M=4.13, SD=1.455), t(15)=4.899 p=0.000

- How tiring was it to use the iPhone? Scale of 1-7 (1: not acceptable, 7: acceptable)

  The difference variable for the acceptance of tiredness for iPhone and laser-pointing device D(16)=0.33, p=0.000, was significantly non-normal.
  The acceptance of tiredness for iPhone (Mdn=7) is higher than the laser-pointing device (Mdn=6): z=-2.154, p=0.031, T=6.

6.7.4 Discussion

The outcome of the experiment indicates that the iPhone is better suited for selecting overlapping objects, objects that are small, or objects which are at a distance. Although it was hypothesized that the laser-pointing device might be quicker than the iPhone to select big-sized objects, the Paired Samples T-test did not prove any significant difference between the two.

Transferring one object from one display to another was significantly quicker using the iPhone, although the researchers had assumed the opposite. The reason behind this outcome might be that it is quicker to point to an object of interest using the iPhone, given that it is enough to move the device in the direction of the display for all the objects to be shown on the iPhone, ready to be selected by a simple tap. The same task with the laser-pointing device might take more time since the user has to point exactly at the object and push the selection button at the same time. The same reason may have influenced the results of the selection of the big-sized objects.

Surprisingly, transferring more objects from one display to two other displays was not quicker with the iPhone. In fact, the result of the T-test showed no significant difference. It was expected that the iPhone would be quicker in performing more complex tasks, where several tasks are done one after another given that the iPhone has a clipboard which can save the selected objects and which the user can carry around. This assumption might be correct, but the experiment used could not prove it, since it was not complex enough. All three displays were located next to each other, so that the user did not have to move to the other side of the room to interact with the other displays.

6.7.5 Limitations of the Interaction Technique

Scalability

The maximum number of objects on each display was:

$$48 = 8(columns) \times 6(rows)$$

Although scalability issues are beyond the topic of this research, some suggestions to this problem are the following.

- Sliding the screen of the iPhone to the left, right, up, and

6.7 Experiment 2: Input Devices Battle

down can extend the number of possible objects to:

$$240 = 5(left + right + up + down + middle) \times 48(objects)$$

In this case selecting any image would take a maximum of two steps, namely sliding to find the correct screen and then tapping on the correct object.

- The iPhone can display the 48 nearest neighbors to the position of the cursor, that is moving the cursor inside a display would update the iPhone's screen continuously. With this solution, it is possible to view all the objects, but just part of them at a time. As mentioned in chapter 4, this can lead to problems, since any small movements of the device would update the GUI of the iPhone.

Multi-User Control

The application can be controlled only by one user at a time. For scenarios such as a brainstorming session, one iPhone per user is useful, so that all the participants have an equal control to create and manipulate the data. Therefore, in the next prototype the application was extended, so that two users can use two iPhones and interact simultaneously (see chapter 7 for more details).

Objects on the Display

In the first experiment, all the objects are considered to be of the same size. Factors such as, relative sizes of the objects, graphical similarity between the objects can be considered in future experiments.

Visual Discriminability

The number of objects that can be shown on the iPhone are dependent on the graphical representation of the objects and the degree of discriminability. In brainstorming applications (see chapter 7), that the objects on the display are some post-its, the size of the icon on the iPhone have to be bigger, in order to be readable and distinguishable for the users.

6.8 Summary of the Chapter

The design and implementation of this prototype show the HCI community the advantages of using a mobile input device with an integrated display for cross-display interaction selection and object-transfer tasks. The first experiment showed that among three potential GUIs for the iPhone, (namely, CoverFlow, DisplayMap, and ZoomGrid), ZoomGrid was preferable and quicker.

The second experiment compared two remote mobile devices, namely a laser-pointing device and an iPhone as representative devices without and with an integrated display. The result of the experiment showed that for these tasks, the iPhone was significantly quicker than the laser-pointing device, when it came to selecting overlapping objects, small-sized objects on two large displays, and transferring one object from one display to another. The experiment could not indicate any significant difference between these two input devices when selecting big-sized objects on two displays, and when transferring more objects from one display to two other displays.

Chapter 7

MDE's Application Domain

> *"The standard engineering design process produces a fundamental blindness to the domains of actions in which the customers of software live and work."*
>
> —Peter Denning and Pamela Dargan, in *Bringing Design to Software*, edited by Terry Winograd, 1996

In this chapter, a few applications for multi-display environments are introduced. One application domain, which is brainstorming meetings, is implemented within the scope of this research. Furthermore, the interaction design process of this brainstorming prototype is highlighted.

7.1 Application Scenarios

Baldonado et al. [2000] investigated benefits of multiple views. They concluded as follows.

"The presence of diversity is one of the foremost reasons for designing a multiple view system."

They consider offering multiple views as useful when one of the following diversity aspects is available:

- Attributes: for example, presenting Google earth for geographical information vs. statistical information via diagrams and scatter plot

- Models: logical structure vs. geometrical layout, hardware vs. software visualizations

- User profiles: preferences, levels of expertise, roles (doctor vs. assistants)

- Levels of abstraction: for example, a detailed view of a map vs. an overview map of metropolitan

- Genres: for example, a block diagram vs. pseudo-code views of a software module

Therefore, multi-display environments are beneficial in several application domains. A few application domains are listed below.

- Home environment: technology at home is a field which has been investigated by many researchers, for example, the Cristal project [Seifried et al., 2009].

- Collaborative programming: for example, IMPROMPTU project [Biehl et al., 2008]

- Meeting rooms: for example, to discuss scientific results, such as Deskotheque project [Pirchheim et al., 2009] for biologists, WeSpace project [Wigdor et al., 2009] for astrophysicists, the multi-user, multi-display prototype based on Google Earth by Forlines et al. [2006] and brainstorming sessions.

The application domain for brainstorming sessions is discussed in the following section.

7.2 Brainstorming

Another field that multiple displays can support is brainstorming meetings, where people gather to find ideas to solve a specific problem. There are different methods to gather ideas. One of the tools that enable electronic idea sharing is Team Storm. Team Storm is a tool developed by Hailpern et al. [2007]. It supports idea generation and information sharing between designers. Each designer has a tabletPC and can share sketches with other people on a large vertical display (see figure 7.1 below).

Figure 7.1: This picture shows an interactive room, where designers can sketch their ideas on their tabletPC, using the Team Storm tool. They can then share these ideas on the large display with other colleagues and discuss them (reference: [Hailpern et al., 2007]).

One of the methods of brainstorming is by using post-its. Hilliges et al. [2007] built an electronic brainstorming prototype, which uses a large vertical display and a touch table (see figure 7.2 below). Users can draw a square with their digital pen on the touch table and in this way generate a post-it.

In this research a prototype based on the post-its method is implemented, which is called CrossStorm. This prototype uses the PrIME prototype concept (see section 6.2 in chapter 6) and implementation as a basis in a real-life application for brainstorming. The traditional metaphor of post-its is digitalized and can be written using the virtual keyboard of an iPhone. More details about this prototype is presented in the following section.

7.3 CrossStorm Prototype

CrossStorm is a PrIME-based prototype that supports users to write digital post-its and post them on different displays. Users can make, delete, and move the post-its across displays. The interaction technique is explained by means of a scenario as follows.

Figure 7.2: This picture shows the electronic brainstorming system which was developed by Hilliges et al. [2007]. Users can create a post-it on the touch table by drawing a square. The created post-its can be clustered and discussed on the vertical display.

7.3.1 Interaction Scenario

Suppose the CrossStorm prototype has no name yet. Two users are invited to brainstorm ideas and come up with a proper name for this prototype. First of all, a moderator explains the problem and writes some keywords that are relevant to the prototype on the Citron display (see figure 7.3 below).

The moderator can write a post-it by clicking on the + button at the right bottom side of the iPhone screen (see figure 7.4 below). Then an editor opens the post-it for writing and the moderator writes Multi-Display environment (see figure 7.6 below). The editor can choose the color of the post-it from the palette on the right side or click the brush button to draw on the post-it (see figure 7.7 below).

To post the post-it to a specific display, the moderator turns the iPhone in the direction of the display and clicks on the tick button on the right side. When the moderator has finished writing the keywords, she explains them and invites the users to write their ideas on post-its and post them on the vertical large display on the right side (Eyevis Cube display). Each of the users have an iPhone (see the iPhones in figure 7.8 below) and start writing

7.3 CrossStorm Prototype

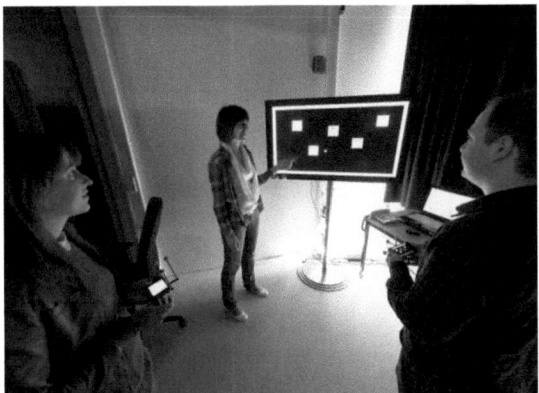

Figure 7.3: This picture shows a brainstorming session using the CrossStorm prototype. The moderator is explaining the problem.

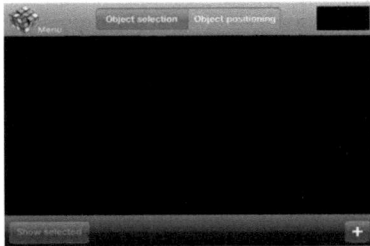

Figure 7.4: This screenshot shows the GUI of the iPhone in the CrossStorm prototype, as it is directed to an empty display. Clicking on the + button at the bottom right side of the screen opens a post-it editor where a post-it can be created (see figure 7.7 below).

names they can think of (see figure 7.9 below).

As soon as the users finish writing their suggestions, they start discussing the ideas and order the post-its on the Cube display on different categories. To order the post-its on the same display, the moderator selects the "object positioning" tab. In this mode, the moderator can see the relative positions of the post-its as they are on the original large display (see figure 7.16 below).

134   7   MDE's Application Domain

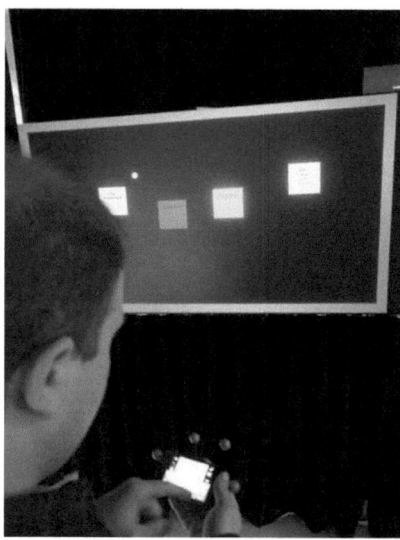

Figure 7.5: This picture shows a user while using the CrossStorm prototype. The user is generating a post-it using an iPhone (the iPhone GUI is shown in figures 7.6 and 7.7 below).

Moving an object within its display is done by putting a finger on the post-it and dragging it to the target position (see figure 7.17 below). Finally they decide on two suggestions and transfer these two post-its to the third display (Microsoft Surface) in order to discuss their decision with the moderator. To transfer the post-its to another display, the users select the two post-its on the iPhone by tapping on them (see figure 7.11 below), and then select the Menu item on the top left side of the iPhone screen. The Object Transfer item is selected and then the iPhone has to be moved in the direction of the target display. As the pointer moves to the Surface, an icon of the Surface is shown on the left bottom left side of the iPhone screen (see figure 7.12 below). Clicking on this display icon pastes the post-it at the position of the pointer. Finally the users and the moderator gather around the Surface, discuss the last two suggestions and decide on one (see figure 7.15 below).

7.3 CrossStorm Prototype

Figure 7.6: CrossStorm prototype: a screenshot of the iPhone GUI for writing post-its.

Figure 7.7: CrossStorm prototype: a screenshot of the iPhone GUI for writing post-its. The editor provides functions, such as choosing the color of the post-it, choosing the brush button to draw on the post-it, canceling the action, and posting the post-it to a display on which the user is currently focusing.

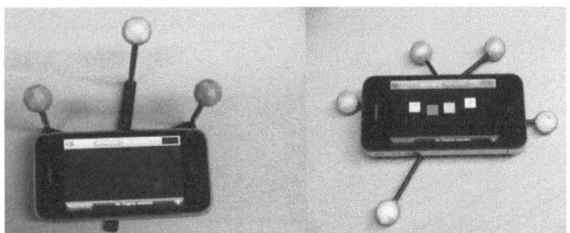

Figure 7.8: This picture shows the two iPhones that were used in CrossStorm as input devices for cross display interaction. Markers are attached to the iPhone, in order to track the device position and orientation in the interactive room.

7.3.2 Design Decisions

The UI design is decided according to the lessons learned from the PrIME experiments. The result showed that the ZoomGrid and the DisplayMap visualizations are faster and preferred more by users. Therefore, these two were selected for the brainstorming prototype. DisplayMap was used for positioning objects within one display, since this visualization presents the relative positions of the objects on the original display and it also helps users to move an object inside its display only by dragging

7 MDE's Application Domain

Figure 7.9: CrossStorm scenario: users are writing their ideas as post-its using their iPhone. The post-it is posted to the large vertical display, as the users click on the 'done' button.

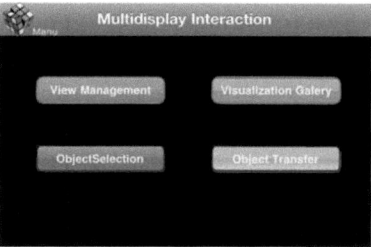

Figure 7.10: This is a screenshot of the Menu items. The Object Transfer Menu enables the user to transfer post-its across displays.

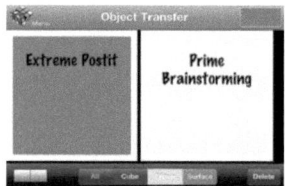 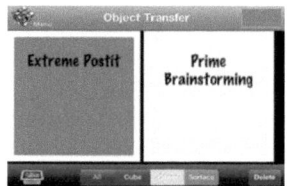

Figure 7.11: Two objects are selected by the user per simple tapping with the finger. The icon on the bottom left side shows the current display which is on focus. In this case, it is the Cube display.

Figure 7.12: Two objects are selected by the user per simple tapping with the finger. The icon on the bottom left side shows the current display which is on focus. In this case, it is the Microsoft Surface.

7.3 CrossStorm Prototype

Figure 7.13: The selected post-its are highlighted on the large vertical display with a white frame around them. Therefore, other users can see which post-its are currently under manipulation.

it around on the iPhone screen, using one finger. ZoomGrid is used to select objects and transfer them to another display, as is used in experiment 2 (see section 6.7).

7.3.3 Advantages of the System

One advantage of this digital system is that information can be saved and stored. Searching large amounts of data is also much easier when the data is digital.

In addition to these standard advantages of digital versus analogue data, CrossStorm allows the generation of ideas anonymously. If several people write and post different post-its in parallel, no one can recognize who has written which post-it. This can encourage people to post their ideas without hesitation. As discussed by Hilliges et al. [2007], anonymity reduces the evaluation apprehension. Another advantage of the system is that people can post ideas at the same time. Hilliges et al. [2007] also concluded that parallelism overcomes production blocking and therefore increases the productivity of brainstorming (see figure 7.18 below). Furthermore, when users write on a post-it, no other members can see what they are writing. As soon as the users are sure about the formulation of their text, they can

7 MDE's Application Domain

Figure 7.14: This picture shows the Media Room at the University of Konstanz, where three users are using CrossStorm for their brainstorming session. Three large displays are being used, namely an Eyevis Cube display, a Microsoft Surface, and a Citron display. 12 tracking cameras are installed in the room in order to achieve the position and direction of the device.

post it for the public to view their idea. This helps the users to concentrate on their individual task without any interruptions.

7.3.4 Future Work

CrossStorm is developed only to show that the abstract concept of the PrIME prototype is applicable in real-life applications. In order to improve the prototype as a tool for brainstorming meetings, some issues have to be considered. Regarding CSCW (Computer Supported Cooperative Work) issues, methods have to be implemented to support synchronization between iPhones. For example, when more iPhones are manipulating the same post-it, the latter has to be blocked till the first user is finished with manipulations.

As assumed in PrIME experiments, the maximum number of objects on one display is 48. One can think of methods to scale the system for more objects. Possible solutions to this problem

7.3 CrossStorm Prototype

Figure 7.15: CrossStorm scenario: the moderator and two users are gathered around the Surface and are deciding on a proper name for the prototype.

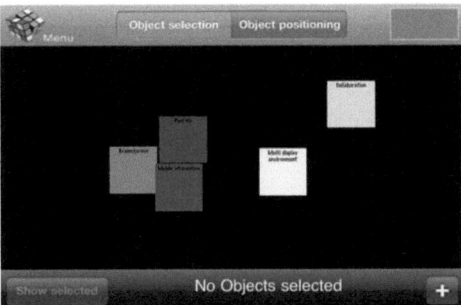

Figure 7.16: This screenshot shows the iPhone GUI in the CrossStorm prototype. The object positioning mode is currently selected where, based on the DisplayMap visualization, the relative positions of the objects are presented, as they are positioned on the large display.

are discussed in chapter 6 of this research. Furthermore, the context of usage plays a role in the number of objects that are presented on ZoomGrid in one page. In experiment 1, 48 abstract colorful shapes were recognizable on one page of the iPhone GUI. In CrossStorm up to 8 post-its are readable on one page (see the mockup in figure 7.19). The decision for the number of objects in one page has to be taken according to the application domain.

140   7   MDE's Application Domain

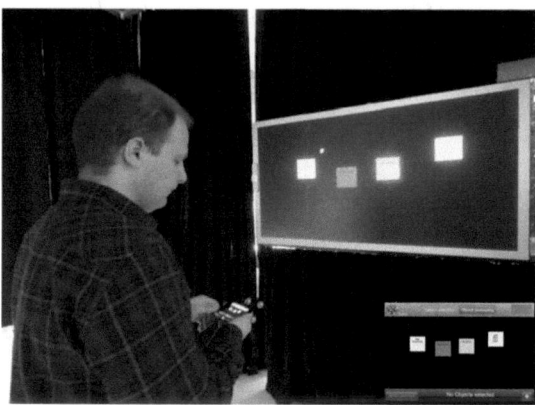

Figure 7.17: The user is interacting with the large vertical display, using an iPhone. As the user points to this display, all the objects are shown in a small form on the iPhone screen. Tapping on the post-its on the iPhone, selects the post-it. The screenshot of the iPhone is presented on the right bottom side.

The important point is that the size of the post-its has to be big enough, so that they are distinguishable from each other.

The DisplayMap visualization which is applied in the Object Positioning mode of CrossStorm, presents the relative positions of the objects as they are shown on the original display. The control to display ratio is not a one-to-one mapping, therefore, an exact positioning of the objects on the large display is not possible in this version of the prototype. This causes different representation of data on the original display and on the iPhone screen in a way that two objects are positioned close to each other on the large display, even though they overlap on the iPhone screen. One solution to this problem is to use a fisheye function and let the user fine-position the objects by zooming in.

Additionally, the GUI of the iPhone has to be adapted to the resolution of the original display. In the above mentioned scenario, The Cube and Citron displays have a 16 * 9 presentation format, but Surface has a 3 * 4 format.

A complete brainstorming tool needs extended features for

7.3 CrossStorm Prototype

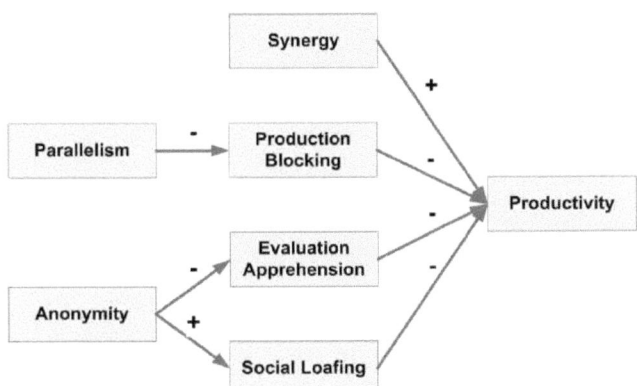

Figure 7.18: This diagram shows the factors that influence brainstorming productivity (reference: [Hilliges et al., 2007]). According to this diagram, the parallelism and anonymity of the CrossStorm Prototype can increase brainstorming productivity. If anonymity bears the danger of social loafing, according to Kerr and Brunn [1983], its benefits appear to outweigh the losses.

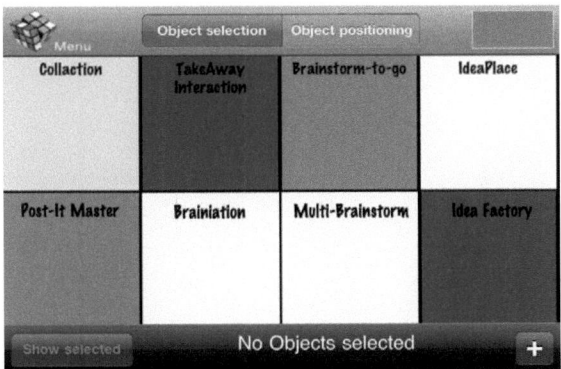

Figure 7.19: This mockup shows 8 post-its on the iPhone. This number of post-its is still readable for the users. More number of post-its in one screen might need the user to zoom in.

drawing, as well as choice of colors, text format and text size.

7.4 Summary of the Chapter

This chapter presented a few application domains, for which multiple displays can be beneficial. Additionally, a working prototype is introduced, which is based on the PrIME prototype. This prototype supports users in brainstorming sessions. Users can write and post post-its using an iPhone. The advantages and disadvantages of the system were discussed above.

Chapter 8

Thesis Conclusions and Future Work

> "Science is always wrong. It never solves a problem without creating ten more."
>
> —George Bernard Shaw

8.1 Conclusion

Both the practical and theoretical aspects of this research focused on Primitive Interaction Tasks for Multi-Display Environment, called PrIME.

8.1.1 Practical Contribution

For the practical part, this research investigated the impact of an integrated display in remote mobile input devices in a Multi-Display Environment (MDE). The research question was as follows.

Does a mobile input device with an integrated display improve performing cross-display interaction tasks?

A user study was carried out to answer this research question by comparing two devices, one of which has an integrated display (an Apple iPhone) whereas the other does not (a laser-pointing device). The outcome of the experiment indicated that the iPhone is better suited for selecting overlapping objects, objects that are small, and objects which are at a distance. Although it was hypothesized that the laser-pointing device might be quicker than the iPhone to select larger objects, the Paired Samples T-test did not prove any significant difference between the two.

Transferring one object from one display to another was significantly quicker using the iPhone, although the researchers had assumed the opposite. The reason behind this outcome might be that it is quicker to point to an object of interest using the iPhone. It is enough to move the device in the direction of the display for all the objects to be shown on the iPhone, ready to be selected by a simple tap. The same task with the laser-pointing device might take more time, since the user has to point exactly at the object and push the selection button at the same time. The same reason may have influenced the results of the selection of the larger objects.

Surprisingly, transferring more objects from one display to two other displays was not quicker with the iPhone. In fact, the result of the t-test showed no significant difference. It was expected that the iPhone would be quicker in performing more complex tasks, where several tasks are done one after another given that the iPhone has a clipboard which can save the selected objects and which the user can carry around. This assumption might be correct, but the experiment used could not prove it, since it was not complex enough. All three displays were located next to each other, so that the user did not have to move to the other side of the room to interact with the other displays.

The subjective feedback of the users showed that the iPhone was considered significantly better than the laser-pointing device. This is because it was regarded easier to use, more accurate for object selection, less tiring to carry and responded quicker to the users input.

Another question which was investigated in this research was:

8.1 Conclusion

Using an iPhone as an input device to control a large display, which GUI and which ordering algorithm would be the fastest and most preferable for the users?

Three different visualizations for iPhone were compared, namely CoverFlow, ZoomGrid and DisplayMap. For each of these visualizations, except for the DisplayMap, different algorithms were used to put objects in order. Therefore, each user tested seven different conditions (DisplayMap + 3 * CoverFlow + 3* ZoomGrid). As the result of the experiment indicated, CoverFlow visualization is significantly slower than the other two GUIs, therefore, it is not appropriate for these sort of tasks.

Although the users practiced zooming to enlarge objects with two fingers, they preferred avoiding this action during the task. They believed that zooming was one of the failures of the GUI as the latter did not present objects which are big enough and so they had to zoom in to be able to select an object.

CoverFlow was not preferred by the users. They thought it was slow when it came to selecting objects, and also that one could only see 9 objects at a glance. In addition, only the object located in the middle of the view is selectable per tap, which means that the user had to swipe further to select other objects.

DisplayMap and ZoomGrid were both similarly fast. In fact, no significant difference was indicated. According to the subjective feedback by the users, the ZoomGrid GUI was preferable, because it showed a good overview of the existing objects. Furthermore, from an interaction designer's point of view, the ZoomGrid has an advantage of using the whole space available on the iPhone screen for presenting the objects. This contrasts to DisplayMap that maps the empty space between the objects from the large display to the iPhone screen. Therefore, users had to slide or scroll less often, and could see a higher number of objects at one glance. ZoomGrid also showed good results regarding the error and coverage rate when compared to the other six GUIs.

The within-subject design of the experiment let all the users try all the conditions. An advantage of this feature was that the users were able to compare the techniques. On the other hand, one disadvantage which was noticed was that the users were not willing to use the zoom option and expected the objects on the display to be big enough for them to see. This happened when they were using CoverFlow and ZoomGrid, but not when using the DisplayMap GUI. The users' opinion might have been different, if the experiment had used a between-subject design approach.

Lessons learned from the design and implementation of these prototypes showed the HCI community the impacts of using a mobile input device with an integrated display for cross-display interaction.

To show the application of the PrIME prototype concept in a real life scenario, CrossStorm prototype was implemented. CrossStorm supports users in brainstorming sessions. Users can make, delete, and move the post-its across displays using an iPhone as an input device. This prototype allowed two users to use two iPhones simultaneously. This gave users the possibility of using more iPhones in order to share their ideas with other members of their group.

8.1.2 Theoretical Contribution

In the theoretical part of this research, a set of primitive cross-display interaction tasks were identified, which, so far, have not been addressed in the literature. These tasks are a good basis for interaction designers, especially to design and evaluate a new input device for MDEs. The primitive interaction tasks are: object selection, object transfer, focusing-brushing-linking in collaborative MDEs and for single-display interaction the visualization gallery primitive task. Furthermore, state transition networks are presented for the primitive tasks based on using the iPhone as an input device.

Figure 8.1 below illustrates the contribution of this research in one glance. The cube shows three dimensions, namely the number of active users, who interact with the system, the number of displays that are controlled and the contribution type. The contribution of this research are divided to three parts of theory, interaction design and controlled experiments. Three prototypes are designed and implemented. This graphic shows the position of these prototypes in the contribution space. In the CloudBrowsing prototype, one active user controlled a single

8.1 Conclusion

display (PanoramaScreen). The PrIME prototype was for single users controlling multiple displays. Finally, the CrossStorm prototype supported multi-user multi-displays.

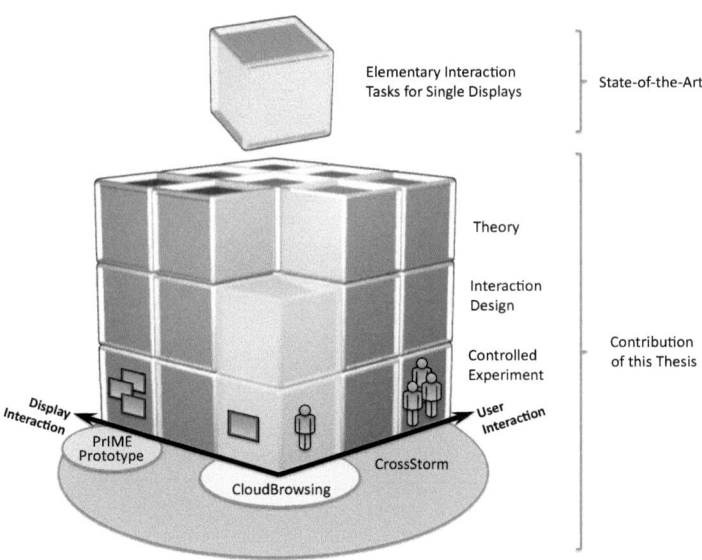

Figure 8.1: This figure illustrates the contribution of this research. The cube shows three dimensions, namely the number of active users, who interact with the system, the number of displays that are controlled and the contribution type. The contribution of this research are divided to three parts of theory, interaction design and controlled experiments. Three prototypes are designed and implemented. This graphic shows the position of these prototypes in the contribution space. In the CloudBrowsing prototype, one active user controlled a single display (PanoramaScreen). The PrIME prototype was for single users controlling multiple displays. Finally, the CrossStorm prototype supported multi-user multi-displays.

8.2 Future Work

There are different aspects that one can build on in order to extend this research further. These aspects are highlighted below.

Extending the List of Primitive Interaction Tasks

Primitive interaction tasks for MDEs (PrIME) are a subset of the whole interaction tasks for MDEs. The main characteristic of the PrIME is that all the interaction tasks can be formed using a sequence of primitive interaction tasks for single displays, and/or primitive interaction tasks for multiple displays. The presented list in this research work is an attempt to achieve this aim and is not guaranteed to be complete. As research in this field makes progress, more primitive tasks might need to be added.

Privacy issues are not considered in the primitive tasks for single or multi-display environments yet. Users should be able to set the privacy rules for each display, for example, which data are viewable to all, who has the right to edit the data. Privacy setting is an option that have to be added to the primitive interaction tasks for single-display environment (PrISE). Furthermore, it has to be considered in the list of primitives for multi-display environment as well, since in a multi-display environment, the relationship between the privacy settings of each two display should be configurable by users. Further research is required to specify what type of interaction tasks should be considered for the privacy issues.

Extending to Further Interaction Primitives

The PrIME experiment 2, which compared an iPhone and a laser-pointing device, tested two interaction primitives, namely object selection and object transfer. The experiment can be repeated in the next stage for other primitive interaction tasks such as visualization gallery.

Mixed Multiple Display and Non-Display Devices

This research focused on controlling devices with a display. The interactive environment can be extended to a mixed multiple display or non-display devices. For example, the iPhone can also interact with a printer inside a room or control devices such as lamps or vacuum cleaners, as was done in the Cristal project [Seifried et al., 2009]

Semantic Relationships

PriME experiments investigated interacting with objects without a semantic relationship. A further research question is: how can the interaction method and object visualization on the iPhone be improved, when the objects are semantically related?

Universal Remote Controller vs. Integrated Member of MDE

The role of the mobile phone in the PrIME and CrossStrom prototypes was as a remote controller. In addition to this role, one can consider the mobile phone as a member of the MDE with a separate display. The stored data in the mobile phone can also be shared with other cooperation partners. Additionally, the result of the discussion can be stored on the mobile phone and taken home.

Attention Management

Attention management in MDE is an important issue. The affordances of the interactive devices should invite the user to interact with them. Furthermore, one of the risks of MDEs is that the user can get confused while interacting with more than one display. Researchers have suggested some solutions to this problem, such as highlighting the displays with LEDs to guide the user where to look. Sound feedback is another solution that can be used to solve this problem. More research is needed in this field, given that an increase in the number of interactive devices in the environment would also lead to this problem becoming more serious.

Appendix A

CloudBrowsing Credits

2008-09 / Research project and interactive installation for PanoramaScreen Bernd Lintermann, Torsten Belschner, **Mahsa Jenabi**, Werner A. König

The interactive installation CloudBrowsing (2008-09) by Bernd Lintermann, Torsten Belschner, Mahsa Jenabi and Werner A. König is the first work to be shown in ZKM's recently established PanoramaLab. The project lets users experience Web-based information retrieval in a new way: Whereas our computer monitor only provides a restricted frame, a small window through which we experience the multilayered information landscape of the Net only partially and in a rather linear mode, the installation turns browsing the Web into a spatial experience: Search queries and results are not displayed as text-based lists of links, but as a dynamic collage of sounds and images. The content-based relations as well as the history of the searches and the information retrieval are not only visualized through the positioning of the individual images that each represent a website, but also through a dynamic soundscape that changes accordingly. In the current version of the project, the user browses the free online encyclopedia Wikipedia, which is compiled by a global community and thus exemplifies the collective knowledge of the Web. A filter mechanism ensures that only open content is displayed in the installation. The cylindrical surface of the PanoramaScreen thus becomes a large-scale browser surrounding the user, who can thus experience a panorama of his movements in the virtual information space.

Bernd Lintermann (*1967 in Düsseldorf) works as an artist and scientist in the field of real-time computer graphics with a focus on interactive and generative systems. The results of his research are used in scientific, artistic and commercial contexts. His computer generated pictures, interactive installations as well as projection environments are internationally presented at festivals and museums. He has been director of the ZKM — Institute for Visual Media since 2005.

Torsten Belschner (*1966 in Freiburg i. Br.) works as sound designer and composer on the interface between music and software. He develops interactive sound installations, which convert complex data streams in multiple-channel environments. Among others, his audio concept, developed for the Bertelsmann Pavillon Planet.m at the Expo 2000 won international recognition as did his audio environment for the interactive installation The Room With a View in the Skoda Pavilion of the VW Auto city, Wolfsburg.

Mahsa Jenabi (*1982 in Teheran, Iran) is a Ph.D. student at the DFG graduate program Explorative Analysis and Visualization of Large Information Spaces and a member of the Human-Computer Interaction Group at the University of Konstanz. Her research focuses on novel interaction techniques for ubiquitous computing environments, specifically multimodal interaction with mobile phones as input devices.

Werner A. König (*1978 in Ravensburg) is a doctoral candidate with the Human-Computer Interaction Group at the University of Konstanz. He is an associated member of the DFG graduate program "Explorative Analysis and Visualization of Large Information Spaces and directs the research project "inteHRDis - Interaction Techniques for High Resolution Displays." His research is focused on the design, development, and evaluation of intuitive user interfaces and input modalities enabling a more natural and reality-based human-computer interaction. Results of his and the group's research are used in diverse domains in science, art, and industry.

A.1 Credits

Visual concept and Panorama software: Bernd Lintermann

Audio concept and audio software: Torsten Belschner, dataphonic audio solutions, Freiburg

Interaction concept and realization: Mahsa Jenabi, Markus Nitsche, Werner A. König

Interface design: Matthias Gommel

The PanoramaScreen is based on Jeffrey Shaw's interactive panoramic cinema research. The PanoramaScreen was jointly developed by the ZKM — Institute for Visual Media, Karlsruhe (D) and the UNSW iCinema Research Centre, Sydney (AUS).

Screen manufacturing: Huib Nelissen Decor en Constructiewerken, Haarlem (NL).

Production: ZKM — Institute for Bildmedien in cooperation with the Human-Computer Interaction Group of the University of Konstanz (D)

Project direction: Bernd Lintermann

Project management and organization: Jan Gerigk, Petra Kaiser

Technical realization: Manfred Hauffen, Jan Gerigk, Nikolaus Völzow, Arne Gräßer, Joachim Tesch

A cooperation project of the ZKM — Institute for Visual Media and the University of Konstanz, Human-Computer Interaction Group (D)

The development of the PanoramaTechnology and the interaction concept was supported by the Information Technology Funding Program of the federal state of Baden-Wuerttemberg (BW-FIT) as well as by the DFG-graduate program GK-1042 "Explorative Analysis and Visualization of Large Information Spaces".

A.2 Reference

State 2009:

http://www02.zkm.de/you/index.php?option=com_content&view=article&id=59

Appendix B

CloudBrowsing Help Instruction

This following picture shows the help instruction for the CloudBrowsing prototype. This instruction was hanging at the entrance of the exhibition room.

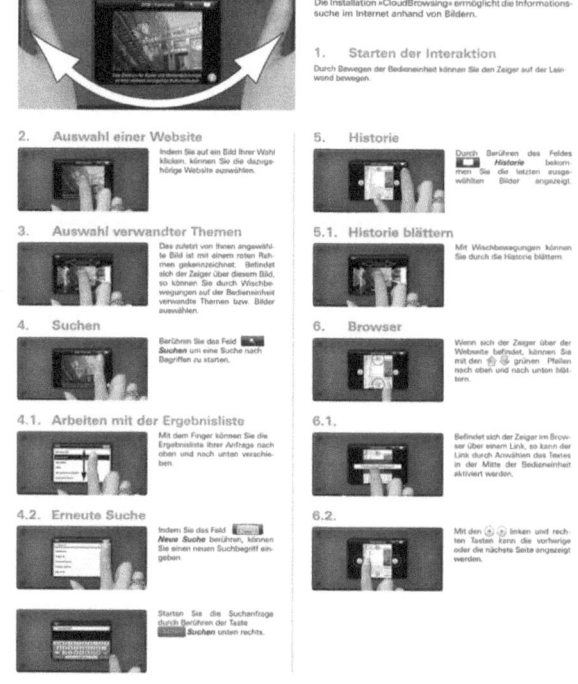

Figure B.1: CloudBrowsing Guidance

Appendix C

PrIME Experiment 2 Tasks

Hypothesis 1: The iPhone is faster than the laser-pointing device for selecting objects that are not recognizable from the user's current position (since they are too small, or the distance between the user and the display is too far.)
Independent variables: Input device (iPhone, laser-pointing device), object size (small, big).
Dependent variables: Interaction speed, user satisfaction

Steps to perform the task: With the laser-pointing device:

- Point the laser pointer to the target display
- Move closer to the display to see the objects better in the case of small-sized objects
- Point to the object of interest inside the target display
- Press the click button on the laser pointer to select the object
- Point the laser pointer to the next display
- Repeat the same steps to select other objects of interest
- Repeat the same steps to select other objects of interest

With the iPhone:

- Point the iPhone to the target display
- Find the object of interest inside the grid
- Tap on the object on the iPhone screen to select it
- Point the iPhone to the next display
- Repeat the same steps to select other objects of interest

Hypothesis 2: The iPhone is faster than the laser-pointing device for transferring multiple objects from multiple displays to multiple displays (order-based tasks). Independent variables: Input device (iPhone, laser-pointing device)

Steps to perform task 1:

With the laser-pointing device:

- Point the laser pointer to display 1
- Point to a blue X inside display 1
- Press the click-button on the laser pointer to select the object
- Press the Menu button on the laser pointer
- Select Object Transfer from the Menu
- Point the laser pointer to display 2
- Press the Menu button on the laser pointer
- Select Paste from the Menu.

With the iPhone:

- Point the iPhone to display 1
- Find the blue X inside the grid
- Tap on the object on the iPhone screen to select it
- Select the Menu button from the iPhone
- Select Object Transfer

- Point the iPhone to display 2
- Select the Paste button from the iPhone UI, by clicking on the display icon on the bottom left side.

Steps to perform task 2:

With the laser-pointing device:

- Point the laser pointer to display 1
- Point to a blue object inside display 1
- Press the click button on the laser pointer to select the object
- Point the laser pointer to the next blue object
- Repeat the same steps to select other objects of interest
- Press the Menu button on the laser pointer
- Select Object Transfer from the Menu
- Point the laser pointer to display 2
- Press the Menu button on the laser pointer
- Select Paste from the Menu
- Repeat the above steps for the red objects

With the iPhone:

- Point the iPhone to display 1
- Find the four red and blue square objects inside the grid and tap on them to select
- Select Menu from the iPhone
- Select Object Transfer
- Deselect the red objects on the iPhone
- Point the iPhone to display 2
- Select Paste from the iPhone UI

- Select Menu from the iPhone
- Select Object Transfer
- Point the iPhone to display 3 (automatically, the red objects are highlighted)
- Select the Paste button from the iPhone UI.

Hypothesis 3: The iPhone is faster in selecting objects hidden behind other objects (overlapping landscape)

Steps to perform the task:

With the laser-pointing device:

- Point the laser pointer to the target display
- Drag the objects aside till the object of interest is found
- Press the click button on the laser pointer

With the iPhone:

- Point the iPhone to the target display
- Find the red and yellow triangles inside the grid and tap on them to select

Bibliography

J. Arvo. *Graphics gems II*. The graphics gems series. Academic Press, 1991. ISBN 9780120644810. URL http://books.google.de/books?id=tQn2pILgt9wC.

Thomas Bader, Astrid Heck, and Jürgen Beyerer. Lift-and-drop: crossing boundaries in a multi-display environment by airlift. In *Proceedings of the International Conference on Advanced Visual Interfaces*, AVI '10, pages 139–146, New York, NY, USA, 2010. ACM. ISBN 978-1-4503-0076-6. doi: http://doi.acm.org/10.1145/1842993.1843019. URL http://doi.acm.org/10.1145/1842993.1843019.

Michelle Q. Wang Baldonado, Allison Woodruff, and Allan Kuchinsky. Guidelines for using multiple views in information visualization. In *AVI '00: Proceedings of the working conference on Advanced visual interfaces*, pages 110–119. ACM Press, 2000. ISBN 1-58113-252-2. doi: http://doi.acm.org/10.1145/345513.345271.

Rafael Ballagas. *Bringing Iterative Design To Ubiquitous Computing: Interaction Techniques, Toolkits, and Evaluation Methods*. PhD thesis, RWTH Aachen University, 2007.

Rafael Ballagas, Michael Rohs, Jennifer Sheridan, and Jan Borchers. Sweep and point & shoot: Phonecam-based interactions for large public displays. In *CHI '05: CHI '05 extended abstracts on Human factors in computing systems*. ACM, 2005.

Louise Barkhuus and Anind Dey. Is context-aware computing taking control away from the user? three levels of interactivity examined. In *Ubicomp 2003*, 2003.

Patrick Baudisch, Edward Cutrell, Mary Czerwinski, Daniel C. Robbins, Peter Tandler, Benjamin B. Bederson, and A. Zierlinger. Drag-and-pop and drag-and-pick: Techniques for accessing remote screen content on touch- and pen-operated systems. In Matthias Rauterberg, Marino Menozzi, and Janet Wesson, editors, *INTERACT*. IOS Press, 2003. ISBN 1-58603-363-8. URL http://dblp.uni-trier.de/db/conf/interact/interact2003.html#BaudischCCRTBZ03.

Jacob T. Biehl, William T. Baker, Brian P. Bailey, Desney S. Tan, Kori M. Inkpen, and Mary Czerwinski. Impromptu: a new interaction framework for supporting collaboration in multiple display environments and its field evaluation for co-located software development. In Mary Czerwinski, Arnold M. Lund, and Desney S. Tan, editors, *CHI*, pages 939–948. ACM, 2008. ISBN 978-1-60558-011-1. URL http://dblp.uni-trier.de/db/conf/chi/chi2008.html#BiehlBBTIC08.

Sebastian Boring, Dominikus Baur, Andreas Butz, Sean Gustafson, and Patrick Baudisch. Touch projector: mobile interaction through video. In *CHI*, pages 2287–2296. ACM, 2010. ISBN 978-1-60558-929-9. URL http://dblp.uni-trier.de/db/conf/chi/chi2010.html#BoringBBGB10.

Harry Brignull and Yvonne Rogers. Enticing people to interact with large public displays in public spaces. In *In Proceedings of the IFIP International Conference on Human-Computer Interaction (INTERACT 2003*, pages 17–24, 2003.

Andreas Buja, John Alan McDonald, J. Michalak, and Werner Stuetzle. Interactive data visualization using focusing and linking. In *IEEE Visualization*, pages 156–163, 1991. URL http://dblp.uni-trier.de/db/conf/visualization/visualization1991.html#BujaMMS91.

William Buxton. Chunking and phrasing and the design of human-computer dialogues (invited paper). In *IFIP Congress*, pages 475–480, 1986. URL http://dblp.uni-trier.de/db/conf/ifip/ifip86.html#Buxton86.

Li-Wei Chan, Ya-Ying Hsu Hsu, Yi-Ping Hung, and Jane Yung-jen Hsu. Orientation-aware handhelds for panorama-based museum guiding system. In *UbiComp 2005 Workshop: Smart Environments and Their Applications to Cultural Heritage*, Tokyo, Japan, September 2005.

Angie Chandler, Joe Finney, Carl Lewis, and Alan J. Dix. Toward emergent technology for blended public displays. In

Bibliography

Sumi Helal, Hans Gellersen, and Sunny Consolvo, editors, *UbiComp*, ACM International Conference Proceeding Series, pages 101–104. ACM, 2009. ISBN 978-1-60558-431-7. URL http://dblp.uni-trier.de/db/conf/huc/ubicomp2009.html#ChandlerFLD09.

Alan J. Dix, Janet Finlay, and Gregory D. Abowd. *Human-computer interaction*. Pearson Prentice-Hall, Harlow [u.a.], 3. ed. edition, 2004. ISBN 0-13-046109-1.

Mike Eissele, Simon Stegmaier, Daniel Weiskopf, and Thomas Ertl. Orientation as an additional User Interface in Mixed-Reality Environments. In Müller, Stefan and Brunnett, Guido and Goebel, Martin, editor, *1. Workshop Erweiterte und Virtuelle Realität*, pages 79–90. GI-Fachgruppe AR/VR, 2004.

Christos Faloutsos and Shari Roseman. Fractals for secondary key retrieval. In *Proceedings of the eighth ACM SIGACT-SIGMOD-SIGART symposium on Principles of database systems*, PODS '89, pages 247–252, New York, NY, USA, 1989. ACM. ISBN 0-89791-308-6. doi: http://doi.acm.org/10.1145/73721.73746. URL http://doi.acm.org/10.1145/73721.73746.

Andy Field. *Discovering Statistics Using SPSS*. Sage Publications, 2009.

Matthias Finke, Anthony Tang, Rock Leung, and Michael Blackstock. Lessons learned: game design for large public displays. In *Proceedings of the 3rd international conference on Digital Interactive Media in Entertainment and Arts*, DIMEA '08, pages 26–33, New York, NY, USA, 2008. ACM. ISBN 978-1-60558-248-1. doi: http://doi.acm.org/10.1145/1413634.1413644. URL http://doi.acm.org/10.1145/1413634.1413644.

James D. Foley, Victor L. Wallace, and Peggy Chan. The human factors of computer graphics interaction techniques. *IEEE Computer Graphics and Applications*, 4(11):13–48, 1984. ISSN 0272-1716.

Clifton Forlines, Alan Esenther, Chia Shen, Daniel Wigdor, and Kathy Ryall. Multi-user, multi-display interaction with a single-user, single-display geospatial application. In Pierre Wellner and Ken Hinckley, editors, *UIST*, pages 273–276. ACM, 2006. ISBN 1-59593-313-1. URL http://dblp.uni-trier.de/db/conf/uist/uist2006.html#ForlinesESWR06.

Jens Gerken, Hans-Christian Jetter, Michael Zöllner, Michael Mader, and Harald Reiterer. The concept maps method as a tool to evaluate the usability of apis. In *to appear in CHI'11: Proceedings of the 29th international conference on Human factors in computing systems*. ACM Press, May 2011.

Vicki Ha, Jim Wallace, Ryder Ziola, and Kori Inkpen. My mde: configuring virtual workspaces in multi-display environments. In Gary M. Olson and Robin Jeffries, editors, *CHI Extended Abstracts*, pages 1481–1486. ACM, 2006. URL http://dblp.uni-trier.de/db/conf/chi/chi2006a.html#HaWZI06.

Joshua Hailpern, Erik Hinterbichler, Caryn Leppert, Damon Cook, and Brian P. Bailey. Team storm: demonstrating an interaction model for working with multiple ideas during creative group work. In *Proceedings of the 6th ACM SIGCHI conference on Creativity & cognition*, C&C '07, pages 193–202, New York, NY, USA, 2007. ACM. ISBN 978-1-59593-712-4. doi: http://doi.acm.org/10.1145/1254960.1254987. URL http://doi.acm.org/10.1145/1254960.1254987.

Antonio Haro, Koichi Mori, Vidya Setlur, and Tolga Capin. Mobile camera-based adaptive viewing. In Mark Billinghurst, editor, *MUM*, volume 154 of *ACM International Conference Proceeding Series*, pages 78–83. ACM, 2005. ISBN 0-473-10658-2. URL http://dblp.uni-trier.de/db/conf/mum/mum2005.html#HaroMSC05.

Mountaz Hascoët. Throwing models for large displays. In Luca Chittaro, editor, *HCI'2003*, volume 2, pages 73–77, 2003. URL http://www.lirmm.fr/~mountaz/Publi/hci03.pdf.

Otmar Hilliges, Lucia Terrenghi, Sebastian Boring, David Kim, Hendrik Richter, and Andreas Butz. Designing for collaborative creative problem solving. In *Proceedings of the 6th ACM SIGCHI conference on Creativity & cognition*, C&C '07, pages 137–146, New York, NY, USA, 2007. ACM. ISBN 978-1-59593-712-4. doi: http://doi.acm.org/10.1145/1254960.1254980. URL http://doi.acm.org/10.1145/1254960.1254980.

Ken Hinckley. Input technologies and techniques,. *Handbook of Human-Computer Interaction*, 2007.

Ken Hinckley, Gonzalo Ramos, Francois Guimbretiere, Patrick Baudisch, and Marc Smith. Stitching: pen gestures that span multiple displays. In *AVI '04: Proceedings of the working conference on Advanced visual interfaces*, pages 23–31, New York, NY, USA, 2004. ACM. ISBN 1-58113-867-9. doi: http://doi.acm.org/10.1145/989863.989866. URL http://portal.acm.org/citation.cfm?id=989863.989866.

Petra Isenberg and Danyel Fisher. Collaborative brushing and linking for co-located visual analytics of document collections. *Comput. Graph. Forum*, 28(3):1031–1038, 2009. URL http://dblp.uni-trier.de/db/journals/cgf/cgf28.html#IsenbergF09.

Shahram Izadi, Harry Brignull, Tom Rodden, Yvonne Rogers, and Mia Underwood. Dynamo: a public interactive surface supporting the cooperative sharing and exchange of media. In *UIST*, pages 159–168. ACM, 2003. ISBN 1-58113-636-6. URL http://dblp.uni-trier.de/db/conf/uist/uist2003.html#IzadiBRRU03.

Mahsa Jenabi. *Selexels: Adapting User Interfaces to Mobile Input Devices*. Vdm Verlag Dr. Müller, 2007. ISBN 383644706.

Hans-Christian Jetter, Werner A. König, Jens Gerken, and Harald Reiterer. Zoil - a cross-platform user interface paradigm for personal information management. In *CHI 2008 Workshop - The Disappearing Desktop: Personal Information Management 2008*, Apr 2008.

Brad Johanson, Armando Fox, and Terry Winograd. The interactive workspaces project: Experiences with ubiquitous computing rooms. *IEEE Pervasive Computing*, 1(2):67–74, 2002. ISSN 1536-1268. doi: http://dx.doi.org/10.1109/MPRV.2002.1012339.

Harry Hochheiser Jonathan Lazar, Jinjuan Heidi Feng. *Research Methods in Human-Computer Interaction*. John Wiley & Sons, 2009.

Rudolph Emil Kalman. A new approach to linear filtering and prediction problems. *Journal Of Basic Engineering*, 82(Series D): 35–45, 1960. URL http://citeseerx.ist.psu.edu/viewdoc/download?doi=10.1.1.129.6247&rep=rep1&type=pdf.

Daniel A. Keim. Information visualization and visual data mining. *IEEE Transactions on Visualization and Computer Graphics*, 08(1):1–8, 2002. ISSN 1077-2626. doi: http://doi.ieeecomputersociety.org/10.1109/2945.981847.

Daniel A. Keim, Christian Panse, Mike Sips, and Stephen C. North. Pixelmaps : A new visual data mining approach for analyzing large spatial data sets. In *First publ. in: Proceedings / Third IEEE International Conference on Data Mining, ICDM 2003 : 19 - 22 November 2003, Melbourne, Florida, pp. 565-568*. Universität Konstanz, 2003. URL http://kops.ub.uni-konstanz.de/volltexte/2009/6974.

N.L Kerr and S.E. Brunn. Dispensability of member dispensability of member effort and group motivation losses: Free-rider effects. *Personality and Social Psychology Bulletin*, 44: 78–94, 1983.

Werner A. König. *Design and evaluation of novel input devices and interaction techniques for large, high-resolution displays*. phdthesis, University of Konstanz, Sep 2010.

Werner A. König, Joachim Böttger, Nikolaus Völzow, and Harald Reiterer. Laserpointer-interaction between art and science. In *IUI'08: Proceedings of the 13th international conference on Intelligent User Interfaces*, pages 423 – 424. ACM Press, Jan 2008. ISBN 978-1-59593-987-6. Demonstration Session.

Werner A. König, Roman Rädle, and Harald Reiterer. Interactive design of multimodal user interfaces - reducing technical and visual complexity. *Journal on Multimodal User Interfaces*, 3(3): 197–213, Feb 2010.

Andrew J. Maunder, Gary Marsden, and Richard Harper. Snapandgrab: accessing and sharing contextual multi-media content using bluetooth enabled camera phones and large situated displays. In Mary Czerwinski, Arnold M. Lund, and Desney S. Tan, editors, *CHI Extended Abstracts*, pages 2319–2324. ACM, 2008. URL http://dblp.uni-trier.de/db/conf/chi/chi2008a.html#MaunderMH08.

David C. McCallum and Pourang Irani. Arc-pad: absolute+relative cursor positioning for large displays with a mobile touchscreen. In *Proceedings of the 22nd annual ACM symposium on User interface software and technology*, UIST '09, pages 153–156, New York, NY, USA, 2009. ACM. ISBN 978-1-60558-745-5. doi: http://doi.acm.org/10.1145/1622176.1622205. URL http://doi.acm.org/10.1145/1622176.1622205.

G. M Morton. *A Computer Oriented Geodetic Data Base; and a New Technique in File Sequencing*. International Business Machines Co, 1996.

Brad A. Myers, Choon Hong Peck, Jeffrey Nichols, Dave Kong, and Robert C. Miller. Interacting at a distance using semantic snarfing. In Gregory D. Abowd, Barry Brumitt, and Steven A. Shafer, editors, *Ubicomp*, volume 2201 of *Lecture Notes in Computer Science*, pages 305–314. Springer, 2001. ISBN 3-540-42614-0. URL http://dblp.uni-trier.de/db/conf/huc/ubicomp2001.html#MyersPNKM01.

Miguel Nacenta, Carl Gutwin, Dzimitri Aliakseyeu, and Sriram Subramanian. There and back again: Cross-display object movement in multi-display environments. 24(1):170–229, 2009.

Miguel A. Nacenta, Dzmitry Aliakseyeu, Sriram Subramanian, and Carl Gutwin. A comparison of techniques for multi-display reaching. In Gerrit C. van der Veer and Carolyn Gale, editors, *CHI*, pages 371–380. ACM, 2005. ISBN 1-58113-998-5. URL http://dblp.uni-trier.de/db/conf/chi/chi2005.html#NacentaASG05.

Jack A. Orenstein and T. H. Merrett. A class of data structures for associative searching. In *Proceedings of the 3rd ACM SIGACT-SIGMOD symposium on Principles of database systems*, PODS '84, pages 181–190, New York, NY, USA, 1984. ACM. ISBN 0-89791-128-8. doi: http://doi.acm.org/10.1145/588011.588037. URL http://doi.acm.org/10.1145/588011.588037.

Christian Pirchheim, Manuela Waldner, and Dieter Schmalstieg. Deskotheque: Improved spatial awareness in multi-display environments. In *VR*, pages 123–126. IEEE, 2009. URL http://dblp.uni-trier.de/db/conf/vr/vr2009.html#PirchheimWS09.

Thorsten Prante, Norbert Streitz, and Peter Tandler. Roomware: Computers disappear and interaction evolves. *IEEE Computer*, 37(12):47–54, 2004.

Roman Rädle. Squidy: A zoomable design environment for natural user interfaces. Master's thesis, University of Konstanz, 2010.

Jun Rekimoto. Pick-and-drop: A direct manipulation technique for multiple computer environments. In *ACM Symposium on User Interface Software and Technology*, pages 31–39, 1997.

URL http://dblp.uni-trier.de/db/conf/uist/uist1997.html#Rekimoto97.

Jun Rekimoto and Masanori Saitoh. Augmented surfaces: A spatially continuous work space for hybrid computing environments. In *CHI*, pages 378–385, 1999. URL http://dblp.uni-trier.de/db/conf/chi/chi99.html#RekimotoS99.

Johan Sanneblad and Lars Erik Holmquist. Ubiquitous graphics: combining hand-held and wall-size displays to interact with large images. In Augusto Celentano, editor, *AVI*, pages 373–377. ACM Press, 2006. ISBN 1-59593-353-0. URL http://dblp.uni-trier.de/db/conf/avi/avi2006.html#SannebladH06.

Thomas Seifried, Michael Haller, Stacey D. Scott, Florian Perteneder, Christian Rendl, Daisuke Sakamoto, and Masahiko Inami. Cristal: a collaborative home media and device controller based on a multi-touch display. In *Proceedings of the ACM International Conference on Interactive Tabletops and Surfaces*, ITS '09, pages 33–40, New York, NY, USA, 2009. ACM. ISBN 978-1-60558-733-2. doi: http://doi.acm.org/10.1145/1731903.1731911. URL http://doi.acm.org/10.1145/1731903.1731911.

Hannah Slay and Bruce H. Thomas. Evaluation of a universal interaction and control device for use within multiple heterogeneous display ubiquitous environments. In Wayne Piekarski, editor, *AUIC*, volume 50 of *CRPIT*, pages 129–136. Australian Computer Society, 2006. ISBN 1-920682-32-5. URL http://dblp.uni-trier.de/db/conf/auic/auic2006.html#SlayT06.

Marc Streit, Alexander Lex, Michael Kalkusch, Kurt Zatloukal, and Dieter Schmalstieg. Caleydo: connecting pathways and gene expression. *Bioinformatics*, 25(20):2760–2761, 2009. URL http://dblp.uni-trier.de/db/journals/bioinformatics/bioinformatics25.html#StreitLKZS09.

Norbert A. Streitz, Jörg Geißler, Torsten Holmer, Shin'ichi Konomi, Christian Müller-Tomfelde, Wolfgang Reischl, Petra Rexroth, Peter Seitz, and Ralf Steinmetz. i-land: an interactive landscape for creativity and innovation. In *Proceedings of the SIGCHI conference on Human factors in computing systems*, pages 120–127. ACM New York, 1999.

Peter Tandler. Software infrastructure for ubiquitous computing environments: Supporting synchronous collaboration with heterogeneous devices. In Gregory D. Abowd, Barry Brumitt, and Steven A. Shafer, editors, *Ubicomp*, volume 2201 of *Lecture Notes in Computer Science*, pages 96–115. Springer, 2001. ISBN 3-540-42614-0. URL http://dblp.uni-trier.de/db/conf/huc/ubicomp2001.html#Tandler01.

Lucia Terrenghi, Aaron J. Quigley, and Alan J. Dix. A taxonomy for and analysis of multi-person-display ecosystems. *Personal and Ubiquitous Computing*, 13(8):583–598, 2009. URL http://dblp.uni-trier.de/db/journals/puc/puc13.html#TerrenghiQD09.

Michael Tsang, George W. Fitzmaurice, Gordon Kurtenbach, Azam Khan, and William Buxton. Boom chameleon: simultaneous capture of 3d viewpoint, voice and gesture annotations on a spatially-aware display. In Michel Beaudouin-Lafon, editor, *UIST*, pages 111–120. ACM, 2002. ISBN 1-58113-488-6. URL http://dblp.uni-trier.de/db/conf/uist/uist2002.html#TsangFKKB02.

Robert Voigt. An Extended Scatterplot Matrix and Case Studies in Information Visualization. Published as Diplomarbeit. Master's thesis, October 2002. URL http://www.vrvis.at/via//resources/DA-RVoigt/DA.pdf.

Mark Weiser. The computer for the 21st century. *SIGMOBILE Mob. Comput. Commun. Rev.*, 3:3–11, July 1999. ISSN 1559-1662. doi: http://doi.acm.org/10.1145/329124.329126. URL http://doi.acm.org/10.1145/329124.329126.

Daniel Wigdor, Hao Jiang, Clifton Forlines, Michelle Borkin, and Chia Shen. Wespace: the design development and deployment of a walk-up and share multi-surface visual collaboration system. In Dan R. Olsen Jr., Richard B. Arthur, Ken Hinckley, Meredith Ringel Morris, Scott E. Hudson, and Saul Greenberg, editors, *CHI*, pages 1237–1246. ACM, 2009. ISBN 978-1-60558-246-7. URL http://dblp.uni-trier.de/db/conf/chi/chi2009.html#WigdorJFBS09.

Xing-Dong Yang, Edward Mak, David McCallum, Pourang Irani, Xiang Cao, and Shahram Izadi. Lensmouse: augmenting the mouse with an interactive touch display. In *Proceedings of the 28th international conference on Human factors in computing systems*, CHI '10, pages 2431–2440, New York, NY, USA, 2010.

ACM. ISBN 978-1-60558-929-9. doi: http://doi.acm.org/10. 1145/1753326.1753695. URL http://doi.acm.org/10.1145/ 1753326.1753695.

Jamie Zigelbaum, Alan Browning, Daniel Leithinger, Olivier Bau, and Hiroshi Ishii. g-stalt: a chirocentric, spatiotemporal, and telekinetic gestural interface. In Marcelo Coelho, Jamie Zigelbaum, Hiroshi Ishii, Robert J. K. Jacob, Pattie Maes, Thomas Pederson, Orit Shaer, and Ron Wakkary, editors, *Tangible and Embedded Interaction*, pages 261–264. ACM, 2010. ISBN 978-1-60558-841-4. URL http://dblp.uni-trier.de/ db/conf/tei/tei2010.html#ZigelbaumBLBI10.

i want morebooks!

Buy your books fast and straightforward online - at one of world's fastest growing online book stores! Environmentally sound due to Print-on-Demand technologies.

Buy your books online at

www.get-morebooks.com

Kaufen Sie Ihre Bücher schnell und unkompliziert online – auf einer der am schnellsten wachsenden Buchhandelsplattformen weltweit! Dank Print-On-Demand umwelt- und ressourcenschonend produziert.

Bücher schneller online kaufen

www.morebooks.de

VDM Verlagsservicegesellschaft mbH
Heinrich-Böcking-Str. 6-8   Telefon: +49 681 3720 174   info@vdm-vsg.de
D - 66121 Saarbrücken   Telefax: +49 681 3720 1749 www.vdm-vsg.de

Printed by Books on Demand GmbH, Norderstedt / Germany